FRANKLIN D. ROOSEVELT
and the
CITY BOSSES

Kennikat Press
National University Publications
Interdisciplinary Urban Series

General Editor
Raymond A. Mohl
Florida Atlantic University

LYLE W. DORSETT

FRANKLIN D. ROOSEVELT
and the
CITY BOSSES

National University Publications
KENNIKAT PRESS   //   1977
Port Washington, N. Y.   //   London

Manufactured in the United States of America

Published by
Kennikat Press Corp.
Port Washington, N.Y./London

Library of Congress Cataloging in Publication Data

Dorsett, Lyle W
   Franklin D. Roosevelt and the city bosses.

   (National university publications: Interdisciplinary urban series)
   Bibliography: p.
   Includes index.
   1. Municipal government—United States—History. 2. United States—Politics and government—1933–1945. 3. Roosevelt, Franklin Delano, Pres. U. S., 1882–1945. I. Title.
JS323.D64   329'.0211   77-2657
ISBN 0-8046-9186-X
ISBN 0-8046-9203-3 (paper)

To Michael, Ted, Erika, and Check

CONTENTS

ACKNOWLEDGEMENTS

The research for this book took me to six states and the District of Columbia. Some of my expenses were paid for by grants from the Penrose Fund of the American Philosophical Society, the University of Southern California, and the University of Denver.

I thank the staffs at the following libraries for facilitating my research: Franklin D. Roosevelt Library, National Archives, New Jersey State Library, Illinois State Historical Society, Memphis Public Library, Holy Cross College, Western Historical Manuscripts Collection of the State Historical Society of Missouri, New York Public Library.

Professor Joseph F. Mahoney, editor of *New Jersey History,* generously granted me permission to use parts of my article on Frank Hague which he published in 1976. I also owe thanks to Professor John Braeman for allowing me to use some of the ideas I expressed on Kansas City for *The New Deal: The State and Local Levels* (Columbus: Ohio State University Press, 1975).

The late Herman N. Weill, former Dean of the Graduate School, Marshall University, helped me begin this study. A long-time friend and colleague, Dr. Weill gave me an interest-free personal loan. This enabled me to take a research trip when I was recently out of graduate school.

Another man who aided me in preparing this book was the late James A. Farley. He gave generously of his time, and answered all of my questions with candor.

Three valued friends read the entire manuscript. Mark S. Foster, Stephen R. Judge and M. James Kedro could not persuade me to erase all of the book's shortcomings, but their critiques helped me improve it.

My chairman, Professor Allen D. Beck, supported my work on this book just as he has every research project I have undertaken since joining the faculty at the University of Denver. Because of his endorsement the Graduate School at the University of Denver paid for typing the manuscript.

My wife, Mary, made a singular contribution to this book. Only she and I know why this book would never have been written without her partnership.

Lyle W. Dorsett
Boulder, Colorado

FRANKLIN D. ROOSEVELT
and the
CITY BOSSES

Lyle W. Dorsett holds a Ph.D. in history from the University of Missouri at Columbia, and has taught at the University of Southern California, University of Missouri at St. Louis and the University of Denver. He has published numerous articles in popular and scholarly journals, and has contributed to books in the U. S. and West Germany. His pamphlets include "The Early American City" (1973), and "Bosses and Machines in Urban America" (1974). He is the author of *The Pendergast Machine* (1968), *The Challenge of the City* (1968), and *A History of Denver* (1977).

INTRODUCTION

For some time now it has been fashionable to attribute the demise of the old-time city bosses to the New Deal. The welfare state, it is assumed, ended the dependence of poor and working people on their favors, and thus brought an end to a long tradition of machine politics. This argument appears in the writing of some of our most respected historians and political scientists, and it emerged as a major theme in a widely read and highly praised political novel, *The Last Hurrah.* Spencer Tracy immortalized the "death of the boss" theme in the film version of this novel, and Rexford G. Tugwell's *The Brains Trust* (1968) reinforced the myth built largely on conjecture.[1] Despite the fact that four case studies have raised serious questions about this thesis, most Americans still hold tenaciously to the belief that Mayor Richard Daley of Chicago was "the last of the old-time bosses," and that the rest of his ilk went down in the wake of the welfare state.[2]

When I started writing this book, my major concern was to make clear that the New Deal did not destroy the bosses and machines. Although this thesis occurs in each chapter, and especially in the conclusion, it gradually became less important to me. I discovered that there was a fascinating story in the relationship that Roosevelt had with each of the city bosses being examined. At first I was bewildered by the lack of consistency in his treatment of and attitudes toward the bosses. Ultimately, however, it became clear that there was definitely a pattern which repeated itself in Roosevelt's dealings with each of the urban leaders. To me that story is more exciting and just as significant as the impact of the welfare state on machine politics, and hopefully it will throw some light on the kind of person who wants to win and retain the presidency.

Another aim of the book is to demonstrate the complexity of boss politics. Too often it is either forgotten or ignored that the words "boss" and "machine" were invented by muckrakers and self-styled reformers during the Gilded Age and the Progressive era. The words connoted wrongdoing and were used disparagingly by people hoping to expose corruption, and by opportunistic "outs" who wanted "in" local politics. Both groups deliberately created a dichotomy with bossism on the one hand, and reformism on the other. This dichotomy, unfortunately, is with us today. It is unfortunate because it is artificial and oversimplified. In fact, there is often strikingly little difference between our so-called bosses and so-called reformers. Fiorello H. La Guardia, for example, was called a reformer, but Ed Crump was tagged a boss. Actually, this distorts our understanding of the political process. Crump was no more evil or corrupt than La Guardia. Both men had efficient political organizations, and both resorted to demagoguery at times. Yet both men ran on reform tickets, and sincerely sought to improve their cities. They were quite successful. Then there was Edward J. Flynn who was denied a diplomatic post because of the stigma of bossism; yet he craved power much less than the highly respected La Guardia, and was much more honest and scrupulous in his political activities than the two self-styled "reformers" Henry Horner and Lloyd Stark, who attempted to destroy bosses Edward Kelly and Thomas J. Pendergast.

A word should be said about the bosses I have selected. No attempt has been made to include the political leaders of every major city. Instead, only bosses with whom Roosevelt was involved most significantly have been included. This criterion limited the number to seven. It is assumed that these seven men and their cities are diverse enough to be a representative sample and to permit some valid conclusions. Geographically the cities range from Kansas City in the West to Boston in the Northeast and to Memphis in the South. The size of the seven cities ranges upward from 270,000 to over 7,000,000. Also, the populations of the cities varied markedly. Kansas City's population was lily-white and native-born, Memphis had a large black populace, and Chicago was composed of native blacks and whites, as well as old and new immigrants.

The bosses, as well as the cities, were strikingly different. They came from varied backgrounds, represented different political parties and viewpoints, and used quite dissimilar techniques to govern their cities. Some were honest and efficient and helped to make their cities better places to live. Others were abjectly corrupt and inefficient. Still others fell somewhere in between. Taking only these marked differences into consideration, one is forced to agree with Harold Zink's thesis in *City Bosses in the United States* (1930) that there is no "typical" boss. On the other hand, if we examine the urban political process we find that all the bosses had something quite fundamental in common: their power depended on serving a wide spectrum of interest groups. Every city embraced numerous groups with interests to protect and goals to attain, and every successful boss had to satisfy the needs and desires of enough interest groups to acquire and main-tain power.

It is often assumed that the bosses had only ethnic minority and working class support. They handed out jobs, food, and clothing to the underprivileged, and in return received loyal sup-port on election day. But this is only part of the picture. To be sure, every successful city boss had support from the lower economic class, but he had to have support from part of the business community and from middle and upper class groups as well. Without a broad base of power no political leader could be more than a mere ward boss or district leader. These men main-tained power throughout their cities with the assistance of people and groups having a wide range of incomes, occupations, and backgrounds. Recognizing the city bosses' diverse support helps explain why the rise of a primitive welfare state could never have been the major reason for the collapse of the big city machines.

1

THE BOSSES
ON THE EVE OF
THE NATIONAL CONVENTION, 1932

There is a touch of irony in the fact that Franklin D. Roosevelt first made a name for himself by leading a fight against Tammany Hall. Before World War I the young state senator referred to the Tammany boss Charles F. Murphy "and his kind" as "beasts of prey." Only twenty years later Roosevelt did everything in his power to gain the support of "his kind," and used them to win and retain the presidency.[1] Although many people were important to Roosevelt's political success, no single group of men was more important to him than the big city bosses; and in the final analysis no other man was destined to be so vital to the life and death of urban political machines as Franklin D. Roosevelt.

This relationship of mutual aid did not materialize immediately. On the contrary, when commitments to candidates for the Democratic nomination were first announced in late 1931 and early 1932, some of the most influential bosses came out in favor of Alfred E. Smith, the party's standard bearer in 1928. Tammany Hall was one of the first organizations to endorse a candidate, and it supported Smith. This was embarrassing to Roosevelt because it meant that his own state would not be united behind him at convention time. On the other hand, it should not have been surprising. The Happy Warrior, after all, was one of Tammany's own. He had gone up through the ranks in the organization, and had brought power and prestige to the Tiger. Al Smith, like many Tammany workers and supporters, was raised in the slums, was of Irish descent, and had been a loyal organization man. Likewise, he was a Wet through and through. And to Tammany's leaders, as to the leaders of most big immigrant-populated cities, ending Prohibition as well as the depression was a major issue in 1932.

The titular head of the Hall was John Curry, the Manhattan chairman since 1929. Although he envisioned himself a shrewd leader and organizer like his predecessor Charles F. Murphy, Curry had little of Murphy's talent. An unusually able leader, Murphy had been Manhattan chairman from the turn of the century until 1924, and the spokesman for the entire Democratic machine in New York City. But Curry was a man of only mediocre ability, and in reality he ruled only his own district. The entire city was actually controlled jointly by Curry and the chairmen of the other three major counties, John H. McCooey of Brooklyn, John Theofel of Queens, and Edward J. Flynn of the Bronx.[2]

All these district leaders except Flynn had backgrounds similar to Al Smith's. They were all poor boys from the slums who had used politics as a means of success. Roosevelt, given his aristocratic background, paled in comparison to Smith in the eyes of these men. Two other circumstances, moreover, made it a certainty that Roosevelt would lose support of New York City's Democrats. One was his refusal to make Prohibition a major issue in his campaign for the nomination. Despite the fact that he knew how important ending Prohibition was to Tammany, indeed to every political machine which counted on Irish or new immigrant support, the governor wanted all New York's delegates behind him at the national convention. Consequently, he could not afford to alienate the Drys, who dominated upstate New York.

The other issue was political corruption, and it directly involved Tammany Hall. In fact, it at least indirectly touched all Tammany's leaders except Flynn. In early 1931 reformers in New York City, led by Rabbi Jonah Wise and the Reverend John H. Holmes, petitioned Governor Roosevelt to remove from office the colorful playboy mayor Jimmy Walker, as well as a number of other Tammany men holding positions in the city government. To avoid offending Tammany, Roosevelt delayed a decision. Finally he did sign a bill prepared by the Republican-dominated legislature which provided a half million dollars for a legislative investi-

gation. As the weeks and months passed, chief counsel for the
investigating committee, Samuel Seabury, uncovered evidence
against suspected offenders. But again the governor refused to
take action. Soon, though, it became apparent that Roosevelt's
efforts to avoid offending Tammany were hurting his reputation
in other parts of the state, and tarnishing his national prestige.
Indeed, Colonel Edward M. House, who had been President
Wilson's advisor years before, warned Roosevelt that his indecisive-
ness was becoming a liability, and predicted that he would never
be elected if citizens outside New York City considered him a
"wholehearted supporter" of Tammany. In less than two weeks
after hearing from Colonel House, the governor removed the first
of several Tammany men involved in graft and corruption. From
that point on, any hope of Tammany support for his presidential
nomination was gone.[3]

While Roosevelt could count on endorsement from many
delegates representing districts outside of the New York City
metropolitan area, only Flynn's Bronx would support him in the
city. The reasons for Flynn's deviant behavior are many. First
of all, unlike many other Irish politicians, he did not identify
strongly with Al Smith. He came from an environment markedly
different from that of Curry, McCooey, and Theofel. Flynn's
father, a native of Ireland, was educated at Trinity College in
Dublin; soon after graduation he married and brought his wife
to America, where they settled in the Bronx. Always comfortable financially, young Ed Flynn dressed and ate well, and was
able to afford the time and expense to get a college education.
After earning a law degree from Fordham in 1912, he soon became a successful attorney.

He entered politics several years later by accident. The Bronx
district leader Arthur Murphy needed a well-known resident to
run for the state Assembly. Flynn was well known through his
law practice in the Bronx, and Murphy asked him to volunteer.
While serving in the state Assembly, and all the time working
diligently for the Bronx organization, he caught the eye of
Charles Murphy. When Arthur Murphy died in 1922, Charles
Murphy elevated Flynn to the Bronx leadership. Six years later
Flynn met Roosevelt, and from then on events conspired to make
them close friends and associates.

When Smith ran for the presidency in 1928, Flynn, by that time one of the influential leaders in the state, supported Roosevelt for governor. The Bronx boss campaigned unusually hard for Roosevelt. Consequently, when Roosevelt was elected he appointed Flynn secretary of state to repay the political debt—and also to get rid of Smith's secretary of state, Robert Moses. Soon after taking his position with Governor Roosevelt, Flynn began preparation for the governor's reelection in 1930. At that point Flynn suggested bringing James A. Farley, a well-known Democrat and the state boxing commissioner, into the campaign. He suggested Farley because the forty-year-old Irishman was bright, outgoing, and liked to travel and talk to people. He already knew the important Democrats in New York. Flynn, in his late thirties, did not enjoy meeting people, shaking hands, and traveling as much as Farley. Always a bit quiet and reserved, Flynn enjoyed reading books and was very reflective. Together, though, they were a perfect team to carry Roosevelt to reelection in 1930 and, with the aid of Louis M. Howe, on to the White House three years later.[4]

Tammany's decision to go for Al Smith was disheartening, but it was only the first of several disappointments Roosevelt would suffer as he moved along the precarious route toward the nomination. His goal seemed still farther away when Jersey City boss Frank Hague announced that New Jersey's thirty-six votes would go to Smith. Hague's choice really was not surprising, inasmuch as he had backed Smith in 1924 and 1928, and was a close personal friend of the man from the lower East Side. And although a booster of Jersey City, Hague always identified with New York City. He had a peculiar habit of having lunch across the Hudson River in New York, a practice he began in the twenties and continued with some regularity until his retirement from politics following World War II. Just how these luncheon excursions began no one knows, but it is tempting to see them inspired through Hague's efforts to be like Alfred E. Smith.

Hague's efforts to pattern himself after the New Yorker make sense if one keeps in mind that when he was still building his own political organization in Jersey City, Al Smith already had entered the governor's mansion at Albany and was well on the way to national prominence. Smith's success especially impressed

Hague because there were only three years difference in their ages, and they came from identical backgrounds. Both men had Irish parents, both were raised in city slums, both entered politics early in life and saw it as the road to status and power.

Despite the fact that Hague had not reached the heights touched by Al Smith, he was an important figure in Democratic politics, and without question the most powerful Democrat in New Jersey. A tall, lean man with sharp features, sandy hair, and piercing blue eyes, Hague arrogantly summed up his role in Jersey City when he snapped, "I am the law." He was the law because he had built an organization in Jersey City and Hudson County which served a variety, indeed a majority, of the interest groups there. In every neighborhood Hague had ward workers serving black, white, and foreign-born minority groups by finding them jobs or helping pay bills. He served the small and large business communities through tax breaks and by cutting the red tape of outmoded zoning laws. A loyal member and large contributor to the Roman Catholic Church, he had its prestigious endorsement at election time. Hague's organization even sponsored social clubs scattered throughout the city to provide lower and middle income people with places to congregate, play, and relax; and even factions of the Republican Party backed him because he traded them jobs for support in primary elections. Once in power, he used his control of the courts and police department to overcome opponents who were too outspoken.[5]

Given Hague's well-organized control of Hudson County and Jersey City, he could deliver a larger bloc of votes than any leader in New Jersey. Inasmuch as he usually was the key to a candidate's victory or failure in a statewide contest, he wielded enormous power throughout the state.

Frank Hague was well known outside of New Jersey, and he attempted to influence Democratic leaders in other states. Months before the Democratic National Convention he tried to convince Chicago's boss, Mayor Anton J. Cermak, to pledge the Illinois delegation to Smith. The mayor, however, would not openly commit himself. Instead, he endorsed Senator James Hamilton Lewis as a favorite son candidate.

Cermak was one of the shrewdest political bosses in the country. Sixty years old, with a receding line of still dark hair, bespectacled and slightly double-chinned, the mayor had come to Chicago in 1889 from Bohemia. Essentially a humorless man, Cermak devoted his life to politics. Gruff, blunt, and virtually obsessed with gaining and holding political power, he devoted every waking hour, usually sixteen or seventeen each day, to politics. He even kept a separate apartment in downtown Chicago where he frequently spent the night, away from his wife, when the demands of politics were most pressing.[6]

Cermak's organization, which embraced all of Cook County, was one of the most diverse and complex in America. Chicago had a total population of approximately 3,300,000, with nearly 1,000,000 foreign born, and almost 250,000 blacks. Not a single minority or ethnic group was ignored or unorganized. Cermak placed Congressman A. J. Sabath, for example, in charge of the foreign language groups. Sabath maintained a publicity bureau with directors for every nationality from the Czechs to the Swedes.[7] The Chicago boss had more than foreign-born citizens' support too. Cermak worked diligently and successfully to win endorsement from the business community. He did so by appointing businessmen to city advisory boards and seeking their advice on many political appointments. Cermak also found widespread support from numerous civic and women's groups because of his welfare programs and campaigns against the underworld.[8]

When Cermak tried to decide whom he would endorse for the presidential nomination in 1932, he had several factors to take into account. Although he was leader of the Cook County Democrats, and for that matter of the Illinois Democrats, he did not rule with an iron hand like Frank Hague. Cermak was power-hungry, yet he was not ruthless and corrupt like Hague. The latter would force people into line with the courts and the police, but Cermak never employed such methods. By refusing to resort to police-state tactics, he found it necessary to "please" the disparaging elements in his motley organization, or face the prospect of desertions.

For example, Al Smith was the favorite of the large and powerful Irish faction of the machine, which Cermak only recently had unseated from control. The Irish faction nevertheless remained within the organization, and the Cermak group did not want to alienate them further. Also, Cermak was an uncompromising Wet (a popular position in Chicago with its large immigrant

population), so he naturally leaned to Smith.[9] On the other
hand, Cermak was not at all certain that when the delegates were
polled Smith could defeat the governor of New York. And the
last thing he wanted was to be on a Smith bandwagon if the Hyde
Park aristocrat won the nomination. To avoid alienating either
candidate, he endorsed Senator James Hamilton Lewis as a
favorite son, hoping to bide his time until it was obvious who
would get the nomination.

Roosevelt and his campaign manager James A. Farley had made
it an inviolable rule not to interfere with favorite son endorsements.[10] Therefore, Farley talked with the Chicago boss, hoping
to convince him that Roosevelt was a good Wet, and get Illinois's
support after the first or second ballot. But the jovial Irishman
got nowhere. Cermak was sympathetic but maintained he was
behind Lewis all the way. Two days after the convention opened,
though, there was a brief moment of optimism among Roosevelt's
workers about winning the support of Illinois, the third largest
delegation at the convention. Senator Lewis withdrew his name,
thus leaving Cermak open to extreme pressures. But the astute
boss was not about to change his plans and be forced into a decision. Instead, he announced that Illinois had another favorite
son, one of his businessmen friends, Chicago banker Melvin A.
Traylor.

This situation encouraged some of Illinois's fifty-eight delegates
to go for Roosevelt on the first ballot, feeling no loyalty to Traylor.
Cermak, who had not forced a unit rule, did not want to railroad
delegates and thereby alienate any factions, so he did nothing.
Most delegates, on the other hand, wanted to stay on the good
side of Cermak, so when the first ballot was cast, over forty votes
were in line for Traylor.[11]

When the votes were counted on the first ballot, Roosevelt
had only 666¼ votes, far from the 770 necessary to win the
nomination. At this point Farley rushed over to Cermak and
asked him to throw all of Illinois to the governor of New York
on the second ballot. Farley felt this would start a bandwagon
for Roosevelt, because he knew Indiana would follow the Illinois
precedent. But again Cermak stalled. He said he was sorry, but
it was necessary for the delegation to caucus before they could
switch, and there was no time before the next ballot. Farley

later commented, "I knew better, but could do nothing."[12]

Up to that point Cermak had played a shrewd game. The Smith forces believed him with them, and the Roosevelt men were uncertain just what he would do. The Roosevelt camp feared the worst, inasmuch as Cermak had packed the galleries with demonstrators, most of whom were pro-Smith. In any case, Roosevelt would have forgiven Cermak if he had started the bandwagon on the second ballot. Farley said:[13]

He [Cermak] had everything in his hands at that moment—national prominence, possibly the Senate which he had his eyes on, and life itself—but he postponed the decision and political opportunity passed him by. Had he jumped to our band wagon then, he would not have been in Miami a few months later seeking political favors only to stop an assassin's wild bullet aimed at Roosevelt.

One man whose delegation had a favorite son, yet played the game in a more open and forthright fashion, was Thomas J. Pendergast, the boss of Kansas City, Missouri. A man who looked almost exactly like the cartoon caricature of city bosses, Pendergast had everything to fit the image except a checkered suit, derby hat, and cigar. He was of Irish ancestry, had pulled himself up by his own bootstraps from a bleak environment, had entered politics quite early in life, and had grown sleek and fat during his years of political success.

Like every powerful political machine, Kansas City's embraced many interest groups. Although the original base of the machine was in the working class neighborhoods where Pendergast's ward bosses provided food, fuel, and clothing for the needy, over the years it spread throughout the city into a motley collection of groups. The most overwhelming support for machine candidates came from the well-organized Irish, Italian, and Negro sections, but this alone was not enough to enable Pendergast to control the city. Indeed, Kansas City, whose chamber of commerce boasted that it was the most "American" city in the nation, had only 6 percent foreign-born registered voters, and blacks accounted for only 10 percent of the total population. Pendergast earned widespread support in middle-income residential neighborhoods because he established poor men's country or social clubs. There folks gathered for picnics and dinners, or bridge games and dances.

Every neighborhood had a baseball team and a bowling league, and these were sponsored by the organization. Pendergast gained strong support from the business community too, because he provided them with fraudulent tax breaks and saw to it that local ordinances which hindered progress or profits were changed or ignored. The Pendergast machine also protected illegal gambling and prostitution, and during Prohibition drinking establishments operated under the aegis of the machine. From these sources the organization received much of the money necessary to maintain its welfare and social services.[14]

During the 1920s the Missouri Democratic Party was faction-torn and weak. Only Tom Pendergast and his Kansas City and Jackson County machine consistently delivered the vote for Democratic candidates. Consequently, by 1932 Pendergast, who had the only well-oiled machine with a large bloc of votes at its disposal, assumed the leadership of the state's party. The Kansas City boss had supported Al Smith in 1928, but in 1932 he unflinchingly came out in favor of Roosevelt.

As early as summer 1931 Pendergast made his position quite clear. He said that if Senator James A. Reed, an old friend and political ally dating back to the turn of the century, "decides to enter the Campaign, I would be required to support him. Secondly, and unless something unforeseen occurs, I will be for Governor Roosevelt, whom I greatly admire."[15] In the early fall Pendergast went to New York and consulted with Farley, Flynn, and Roosevelt. Upon his return he said that he wanted to support Roosevelt, and hoped that Reed would decline to run as a favorite son. A newspaper reporter quoted him as saying:[16]

Missouri would be for Senator James A. Reed to a man if our own distinguished Democrat were to announce his candidacy for the Presidential nomination. We would be for him first, last and all the time. If he does not enter the contest, it looks as if our delegation would be for Governor Roosevelt. That is what I gather from my talks with party leaders. Roosevelt appears to be the popular choice all over the country. He has great strength everywhere, even in Dry States. I feel sure he would carry New York and be elected by a handsome majority.

By the time the convention met in Chicago the next summer, Reed still insisted his name be put in nomination. But far-sighted

Pendergast knew the aged senator did not have a chance of winning. So to help Roosevelt, yet save Reed's ego, Pendergast freed the Missouri delegation from its traditional unit rule. All he asked the delegates to do was cast their votes for Reed on the first ballot, and from there on they were to go for Roosevelt whenever Farley called for help. Pendergast consulted with Roosevelt and Farley about this over the telephone a few days before the convention. The presidential aspirant knew he could count on Pendergast after the first ballot.[17]

It may seem strange that Pendergast, with a background similar to Smith's, preferred Roosevelt for the nomination. Actually, his choice was the only sensible one he could make, because Kansas City, unlike Jersey City or New York, was overwhelmingly native American in population. No doubt, from his viewpoint it was more advantageous to endorse a candidate who avoided making a major issue of ending Prohibition than to risk alienating many voters by backing ultra-wet Smith.

One man who promised to deliver the vote for Roosevelt, but failed miserably, was James Michael Curley, mayor of Boston, Massachusetts. No doubt the most colorful Democrat in the Bay State, Curley was one of the greatest orators of his era. With his sharp, sparkling eyes, his long, pointed nose, tall frame, and slightly potted belly, he could cock back his head, open his mouth, and enrapture listeners by the thousands. But despite his color and popularity, he was not the man of power in the Massachusetts Democratic Party. Although he was often called a boss, he had a poor excuse for an organization, and did not even come close to wielding the power of a Hague or Pendergast.

As J. Joseph Huthmacher has pointed out in his book *Massachusetts People and Politics,* the Irish had dominated politics in Boston since the turn of the century. No real machine or tightly constructed organization existed. Instead, there was a constant struggle between several ward bosses on the one hand, and men with personal followings such as John F. Fitzgerald, Martin Lomassney, and James M. Curley on the other. When Curley ran for public office, which he had done continually since 1900, he had no chance of winning unless he succeeded in forming an alliance with some of the ward bosses and securing the backing of other men with large personal followings.[18] He did have some city patronage which he used to advantage while he was mayor.[19] He failed, however, to organize neighborhoods. And the overtures he made to the new immigrants from southern and eastern Europe were too little and too late. David Walsh and his faction beat him to the punch.

It was astute David Walsh who built a powerful coalition of ethnic minorities (new immigrants as well as the Irish), anti-Prohibitionists, and a discontented laboring class suffering from a decline in the textile and shoe industries. In 1930 Walsh, who had entered the Senate three years before, put his coalition behind the western Massachusetts Yankee Joseph Ely for the gubernatorial nomination. Curley refused to back Ely in the primary. But Ely won, and then went on to win the gubernatorial election. By 1930 Senator Walsh and Governor Ely controlled state patronage and most of the state's federal patronage, and Mayor Curley was isolated.[20]

It was this isolation which encouraged the flamboyant mayor to support Franklin Roosevelt's bid for the nomination. At first glance it would seem strange for Curley to favor Roosevelt. After all, the Boston politico had so much in common with Al Smith. Like the New Yorker's, Curley's parents were born in Ireland; he was forced to quit school and go to work at an early age; and he turned to politics as a means of finding status and financial security. He enthusiastically campaigned for Smith in 1928; both men were unequivocal Wets; and besides, in 1932 most Massachusetts Democrats were for Smith.

Curley, however, had a plan. Always the optimist, and never one to pass up a good political fight, he believed that if he was one of the first on the Roosevelt bandwagon, and if the bandwagon rolled to victory, he would get enough patronage and favors from Roosevelt to build up his own organization and challenge the Walsh-Ely domination of the state Democratic Party.

Curley launched his big gamble in late summer 1931. Using his mayor's office stationery, he sent letters to all Democratic senators and congressmen. He argued that Roosevelt's sweep of New York in the last election proved his immense popularity, and that he should have the party's undivided support. But Curley wanted to do more than merely mention Roosevelt to Democrats; he wanted them to commit their support. Curley wrote: "I take pleasure in enclosing you one of the emblems that the National-Roosevelt-for-President-Club, of Massachusetts, is sponsoring. It bears the slogan, AMERICA CALLS ANOTHER ROOSEVELT. I sincerely trust that it will meet with your personal approval and that you will allow us to enter your name upon our rolls as an honorary member."[21] Curley did not limit his campaign to congressmen and senators, but sent circulars to leading Democrats throughout the nation.[22]

Curley's number-one aide in the Roosevelt-for-President drive was Roosevelt's oldest son, James. The two men worked hard to find supporters in all states, but they labored with extra energy in Massachusetts. During the early weeks of 1932 both men tried to convince Roosevelt that he should oppose Al Smith in the Massachusetts preferential primary. Jim Farley and Louis Howe, who always had their ears to the ground and seldom misinterpreted political rumblings, advised otherwise. They told the governor to stay out of the Massachusetts primary because there was no way to defeat the Walsh-Ely organization, which was 100 percent behind Smith. But after listening to the optimistic pronouncements of Curley and James Roosevelt, and after winning the primary in New Hampshire, Roosevelt decided to enter the fray.[23]

As usual Roosevelt's reliable prognosticators, Farley and Howe, were correct. Smith defeated Roosevelt with ease and won all thirty-six Massachusetts delegates to the national convention. Roosevelt did learn an important lesson from the experience. Curley had no organization of significance in Massachusetts, and he was either the worst political observer in the state or one who preferred to paint a rosy picture of things rather than tell the sometimes unpleasant truth. From that point on Roosevelt would be cordial to Curley, but he would never seek his advice, listen to his analysis of the political situation, or take him into his confidence.

Yet Roosevelt had absolutely nothing to gain by being bitter toward Curley. It was the governor, after all, who made the decision to enter the contest. He wrote an extremely cordial letter to the mayor and thanked him for his efforts.[24] The letter bolstered Curley's optimism. If he continued to work in Roosevelt's behalf, he thought, he could still take over the federal patronage in Massachusetts and challenge the Walsh-Ely control of the state

Democratic Party. Consequently, Curley organized a "Roosevelt Special" train to go to the convention in Chicago. With flying banners the train carrying nearly two hundred Roosevelt supporters left Boston and stopped to pick up the New Hampshire delegation and the Vermont delegates pledged to the New York governor. It stopped at Albany; its enthusiastic passengers got off to hear a speech by Roosevelt; then it rolled on to Chicago.[25]

Another city boss who supported Roosevelt from the beginning, but for reasons far different from Curley's, was Edward H. Crump of Memphis, Tennessee. Memphis, like Kansas City, was a city of mostly native Americans; therefore, Prohibition was not the central issue. Also, Crump liked Roosevelt's style, and his position on major issues; he believed he was the man who could defeat the Republicans in 1932.[26] Despite the fact that Roosevelt was generally well informed when it came to knowing who was in control of the party machinery of each state, he and his staff were surprisingly ignorant of Crump's position and power in Memphis. Indeed, when Crump prepared to organize a Roosevelt-for-President Club, a member of Roosevelt's campaign staff wrote to the Tennessean Cordell Hull, whom they knew and trusted, to ask if Crump's activities would embarrass or hurt them with the men of power in the Tennessee party.[27]

Without a doubt, Crump was one of the most powerful Democrats in Tennessee, and he had been for over two decades. In 1910 he was elected mayor of Memphis on a reform ticket with the aid of a young attorney, Kenneth D. McKellar (who was by 1932 a United States senator and strong Roosevelt supporter). Boss Crump was elected to the United States House of Representatives in 1930, but he still maintained control of his powerful and efficient Memphis and Shelby County machine. According to his biographer William D. Miller, Crump did not want to be considered "as one of the same stripe as Curley of Boston, Hague of Jersey City, or Pendergast of Kansas City."[28]

Like many people, Crump assumed that these three men were exactly alike, as did many people who stereotyped city bosses. The boss of Memphis had many things in common with them, but like every boss, he too was unique. As did Pendergast and Hague, he maintained a powerful, dependable machine. Unlike Curley, he could deliver the vote, but he never resorted to Hague's ruthless tactics to do so. He was never caught stealing money or misappropriating funds like Pendergast. On the contrary, he was praised for bringing progressivism to Memphis by giving it a streamlined, efficient government, and public improvements at the same time.

Ed Crump bore little resemblance to the stereotype of the city boss. In his late fifties by the time he entered Congress, he had bushy, snow-white hair and John L. Lewis-like eyebrows. His black round-rimmed glasses accentuated wide eyes which exuded the seemingly boundless energy for which he was well known. Unlike the other bosses with whom he was often identified, he was not of Irish extraction. His parents were native southern Americans, and his father had served in the Confederate army. Born in Holly Springs, Mississippi, to rather well-to-do parents, he moved to Memphis as a young man. Quite rapidly he became a successful businessman, and he went into politics for the challenge rather than as a stepping stone to status and economic security.

Crump started building his political machine at Memphis in 1910. By the time Roosevelt made his bid for the nomination, Crump had perfected the machine in the city and extended it throughout Shelby County. Crump's machine was similar to other city machines inasmuch as it was composed of a motley assortment of interest groups. It was unique, on the other hand, because immigrant groups did not play a significant part—indeed, they played no part at all. In 1930, for example, the population of Memphis was over 250,000 but only 5,000 were foreign born— quite a contrast when one remembers that almost one-third of Chicago's population was foreign born. Crump's machine did have an underprivileged, lower economic class group to aid, and then to organize—the blacks. The first Democrat in Memphis to exploit the blacks, Crump was willing to receive some criticism from whites in order to win an enormous bloc of votes. Numbering about one-fifth of Memphis's population when Crump entered politics, the blacks comprised over one-third of it by 1930.

Some of Crump's political enemies used the black issue against him at election time. In 1932, for example, a pamphlet was distributed entitled "Edward H. Crump: Public Enemy No. 1." The pamphlet charged that "to Crump the people of Tennessee owe the odium of first bringing the negro into state Democratic politics."[29]

Crump's power, however, was based on more than the black vote. He devoted his life to seeking out the needs of every interest group of significant size, and then doing all he could to provide them with services. He courted leaders among Baptists, Catholics, Jews, and won their endorsement and respect. He became the darling of the business community because he was a respected businessman himself, and because he gave Memphis an efficient government, low insurance rates, and the image of a community on the move which was attractive to outside capital. He also had literally thousands of city and county employees under his thumb, and they made a powerful voting bloc at election time.[30]

Senator Kenneth McKellar, who maintained a statewide organization, was a native of Memphis and a close personal friend of Boss Crump's. Crump's Memphis organization was always aligned with McKellar. Combined, they were a powerful force in the Tennessee Democratic Party. As early as November 1931 the Memphis organization and McKellar gave their commitment to James M. Curley's Roosevelt-for-President organization and endorsed Governor Roosevelt for the Democratic nomination. And true to their word, Tennessee's twenty-four votes went to Roosevelt on the first ballot.[31]

Roosevelt's victory at Chicago found all the big city bosses in a state of turmoil and uncertainty except Pendergast, Curley, Crump, and Flynn. Immediately after the convention the scramble began. Those who had bet on the wrong man did their utmost to get into Roosevelt's good graces. The new leader of the Democratic Party, however, would not be moved by either petty resentments or blind loyalty. As always, he took a cold, narrow view, and rewarded or penalized on the sole basis of how he though it would affect him politically.

2

"THE GREAT ESTRANGEMENT"

JAMES M. CURLEY

Soon after the Smith forces devastated Roosevelt in the Massachusetts primary, Roosevelt wrote a letter to Curley.[1]

Just a line to express to you my heartiest congratulations and warm appreciation for the magnificent campaign you made despite all the obstacles. I realize you had the entire state machine, the two United States Senators and the Governor against you; and that you with Jimmy Roosevelt campaigned the whole state practically single handed and made a remarkable showing. I want you to know that I personally am more grateful than you will ever know for the wonderful fight you put up in the most extreme conditions.

If Roosevelt was grateful to anyone, it was to the gods of power politics for showing him Curley's true colors before he ever relied on the Boston politico's judgment again. Curley, who along with Roosevelt's son James had predicted victory if he would only enter the Massachusetts primary, was either a liar or the worst political observer in the Bay State. Because Curley was an unreliable prognosticator, and because the Massachusetts organization was controlled by Curley's enemies, Senator David Walsh and Governor Joseph Ely, Roosevelt quickly cooled his relationship with the Boston mayor. Indeed, immediately after the convention Roosevelt forgot who had supported him in Massachusetts and went directly to the men of power. Loyalty to political supporters was never important to the Democratic standard bearer. The expedient thing to do in this case was to garner the favor of Walsh and Ely, because without their support he could not carry Massachusetts in the general election.

Senator Walsh, with an eye on federal patronage, immediately responded to Roosevelt's overtures and pledged his support. Walsh also persuaded the junior senator, Marcus Coolidge, to do the same. Governor Ely, on the other hand, who delivered the Smith nomination speech at Chicago, thoroughly disliked Roosevelt and refused to join Walsh. Consequently, Farley went to Massachusetts to see Ely and persuade him to visit Roosevelt at Albany a week later. Governor Ely quite reluctantly made the trip. Afterwards, and without enthusiasm, he agreed to endorse Roosevelt, but on the condition that Curley be relegated to the background, and that the Walsh-Ely organization be allowed to direct the state campaign.[2]

Ironically, then, the man who had gambled and backed Roosevelt, hoping that a victory would give him the edge over Walsh and Ely, was pushed aside soon after the convention. But Curley was always optimistic. Undaunted by the fact that he was not even wanted for speechmaking duty by the Massachusetts organization, he barnstormed across the nation from the East Coast out to Los Angeles, up to Oregon and Washington, and then back east through the major cities of the Middle West, making speeches for Roosevelt everywhere he stopped.[3]

Trying desperately to win Roosevelt's affection, Curley did more than make speeches and pay his own expenses. Between Roosevelt's nomination and inauguration, the mayor of Boston inundated the future president with letters and telegrams. Most of the messages reflected obvious apple polishing, and the phraseology usually exuded hyperbole and sweetness. Curley congratulated Roosevelt on everything—speeches he made to the nation, the work being done at Warm Springs, and the birth of his son Elliott's child. Once he sent a letter congratulating Roosevelt for a speech he made to the nation, and then followed it up the next day with a telegram which repeated the letter word for word. On Roosevelt's birthday in January 1933 Curley sent a telegram and then a book as a gift.[4] And the day after Boss Cermak was shot by a bullet intended for Roosevelt, Curley hurried a telegram which said, "In common with every citizen interested in America I rejoice that Almighty God in His mercy saw fit to preserve you for the good of the people in America from the bullet of an assassin."[5]

Despite his vulgar style and political motives, Curley had worked diligently for Roosevelt's nomination and election. Indeed, with the exception of men such as Flynn, Farley, and Howe, probably no one worked harder in the campaign than James Michael Curley. Justice demanded he receive some reward for his services, but how much of a reward was a subject of debate. Curley always resented the fact that he was not given a share of Massachusetts's federal patronage, but Roosevelt was not about to lose support of the state's only workable machine and try to build a new one from the bottom up.[6] Curley also believed the president owed him a position in the cabinet. As a matter of fact, he maintained in his autobiography that Roosevelt promised he could be secretary of the navy but then backed down when the Senate threatened to investigate Curley's mayoralty administration. Half-apologetically Roosevelt then offered Curley the post of ambassador to France or Italy. The Irish Catholic said he preferred Rome, but once again the president backed down on his promise because of pressures from Curley's opponents.[7]

A month after taking office Roosevelt finally came through with a firm offer to Curley—ambassador to Poland. The mayor of Boston, however, found the position unattractive and the offer insulting.[8] He declined, and from that day on Curley and Roosevelt were at loggerheads.

The Roosevelt-Curley feud was accentuated by Roosevelt's refusal to give Curley any of the federal patronage that went to Massachusetts. Nearly 150,000 federal jobs were handed out in the Bay State, and Mayor Curley did not have a voice in filling even one of these positions.[9] To make matters even less palatable to Curley, many key posts were given to his arch political enemies. Charles Hurley, a Walsh-Ely man who was destined to succeed Curley as governor, was offered the position of deputy collector of internal revenue. John Maynard was appointed to the coveted office of collector of customs. The appointment of Maynard, a staunch enemy of Curley's, was a particularly bitter pill for the mayor to swallow. He tried to get Maynard removed from the post, but to no avail.[10] Roosevelt was finished with Curley. Senator David Walsh was the favorite in Massachusetts now.

Although it was common knowledge among the professional politicians that Curley and Roosevelt were at odds, ordinary citizens were not always so well informed. And as far as Mayor Curley was concerned, there was no need for them to be. When he decided to seek the Democratic gubernatorial nomination in 1934, he wanted to take full advantage of the popularity of both Roosevelt and the New Deal in the state. Curley, after all, had no organization. If he was to buck the Walsh-Ely machine, which was fairly well organized and now had a sizable block of federal patronage at its disposal, he must do so solely by personal appeal to the voters.

Charisma always had been Curley's basis for support. He never had built ward and precinct organizations, let alone a statewide machine in the tradition of the Hague and Pendergast machines. His style was strictly personal, and his popularity among the voters came from public speeches and headline-catching antics. When Curley delivered a well-thought-out and prepared speech, he made it appear as though he was doing it extemporaneously— straight from the heart. He often crashed banquets and rallies where he would appear just long enough to clown it up and say a few appropriate words off the cuff. As city councilman, mayor, and state representative, he seldom delegated responsibilities which would attract the attention of newspaper reporters. Curley spent more time kissing queens at beauty pageants, handing out trophies at fishing contests, and introducing famous personalities than he did drawing up significant legislation.

Occasionally Curley was capable of playing upon the baser feelings of his constituents. He seldom failed to use his Roman Catholicism to advantage in Massachusetts. He frequently identified himself with Church functions and in 1931 managed an audience for himself and his family with Pope Pius XI. After the audience Curley had himself and his family photographed in front of the Vatican and, of course, made sure the picture was well circulated back home with an appropriate notation about their visit with His Holiness.[11]

Curley made a well-publicized visit to Ireland, which had its desired effect on the Irish-Americans. One time he even sent a flag of the City of Boston to Benito Mussolini. The flag had a shield affixed to it, which read: "Presented to the Savior of

Christian Civilization, Benito Mussolini, by the City of Boston, James M. Curley, Mayor."[12] This was politically astute in a state with thousands of first- and second-generation Italian-Americans.

As much a part of the Curley appeal as speechmaking and publicity stunts was identification with men of power and prestige. The Boston politico pulled every string possible to be photographed with important people. It was part of his conscious effort to create an image of himself as a man of the people who also was close to the power elite at home and in Washington. It was in this vein that Curley hoped to take advantage of Roosevelt's popularity. By identifying with Roosevelt and the New Deal, he attempted to add to his large personal following; this was his only chance of defeating the state organization in the race for the gubernatorial nomination.

A key tactic in Curley's strategy was to use James Roosevelt as much as possible in the campaign. Jimmie's name alone was an asset to Curley. When the younger Roosevelt attended rallies in person with the mayor, exuding his blithe spirit and winning smile, he reminded people so much of his father that it could not help but sway those countless voters who venerated the new chief executive.

Inasmuch as Curley needed James Roosevelt's visible support and not his advice, it made little difference that the latter had no political acumen. Indeed, it was probably fortunate for Curley that he was, in reality, politically obtuse. If James Roosevelt had understood Massachusetts politics and had been a good judge of where the power lay, he would never have gotten involved with Curley. But the president's son was first and foremost an insurance man in Boston. Politics intrigued him, so he decided to dabble. He dabbled with Curley because he was the mayor, he was popular, and he delivered just the right amount of flattery.

Certainly Jimmie Roosevelt helped Curley's cause. The majority of the citizens in the Bay State in 1934 were pro-Roosevelt, and most of them assumed that if Roosevelt's son was actively for Curley then the president must be too. Even the anti-Curley people saw it in the same light. And plenty of them sent irate letters and telegrams to the president—instructing him to keep his son's nose out of the Massachusetts primary.[13]

Despite President Roosevelt's misgivings about Curley, and

his realization that the mayor was using his name and prestige, he refused to intervene. His restraint, however, was no doubt purely out of deference to his son. The president's neutrality was the best Curley could hope for during the campaign, and neutrality was the stance the administration maintained. Even James A. Farley, by this time postmaster general, refused to take sides publicly when personally confronted in Worcester during the primary campaign.[14]

Several factors conspired to enable Mayor Curley to win the gubernatorial nomination and surprise the professionals, who believed he could never stop the state machine. First of all, Curley had a sizable personal following because he was a colorful figure with plenty of energy and enthusiasm. Added to his charisma was the popularity of Roosevelt, and he unhesitatingly rode on those coattails. It should be kept in mind that the president was extremely popular during the summer of 1934. Most New Deal programs were just getting underway, and the critics were not terribly noisy yet. Another factor was the overconfidence of the Walsh-Ely organization. They controlled federal patronage; they had walloped Curley in the 1932 presidential primary—how could they lose now? They did lose, though, because the federal workers were not well organized yet, and the state organization did not work hard in the campaign. And finally, Governor Ely made the strategic error of campaigning almost solely on an anti-Curley platform. He smeared Curley by continually reminding the voters he had served time in jail (in 1903) for taking a civil service examination for another man. He suggested, without evidence, that Curley always had his hand in the public till. He followed up this accusation with a dig at Curley's campaign scheme of identifying himself with Roosevelt. "Mr. Curley," Ely declared,[15]

is talking much of his support of and agreement with the principles and policies of President Roosevelt. I would like to ask him if he agrees with the principle of President Roosevelt, enunciated when he was Governor of New York, in the case of Sheriff [Thomas] Farley and that of Mayor Walker, when he said that when men who hold public office like these show evidences of wealth not consistent with the offices they hold and the remuneration which goes with those offices, I believe the responsibility is theirs to show where they got it.

This approach backfired. Most voters found Ely's arguments unconvincing, and they resented the attacks on the mayor's character. Curley defeated his opponent, General Charles Cole, by nearly a two-to-one margin. So, thanks to his own strategy and the help of Governor Ely's abortive speeches, the Walsh-Ely machine was upset.

After the election journalists heralded Curley as the new leader of New England's Democrats—a revolutionary who had taken control of the Bay State. But these were superficial observations. Curley went on to the governor's mansion after the November elections because Senator Walsh decided to support the entire Democratic ticket on the stump, and so did the tireless campaigner and speechmaker James A. Farley. And 1934 was a Democratic year all over the country.

Governor Curley was unable to solidify this victory into anything that even resembled permanence. An indication of his inherent weakness was the fact that he defeated his Republican opponent by only slightly more than 100,000 votes, whereas David Walsh, who ran for reelection as senator, won by over 300,000 votes. Walsh not only proved to be a much stronger vote getter in the state at large, he even outpolled Curley in Boston.

James Michael Curley's residence in the governor's mansion did not give him control of the state organization. He had never been good at building machines. Walsh, on the other hand, was extremely adept at this. He obviously was more popular than Curley, and he refused to make peace. In Washington the feeling was strong that Curley was still a loser—one who had walked into the state house by accident and probably wouldn't be there more than one two-year term. Louis M. Howe was still down on the new governor. He viewed him as an inefficient politico who failed to keep promises.[16] Although Roosevelt saw Curley once after the election, their relationship was strained. Nothing really had changed.

The determination of Washington to support David Walsh strained the Roosevelt-Curley relationship still more. The New Dealer continued to funnel patronage and monetary plums through the senior senator rather than through the governor. Curley was furious. He complained that in December 1934 he had an appointment to see Harry Hopkins, who was in charge of federal relief programs. Curley obviously hoped to win some of the patronage away from Walsh, but Hopkins refused to keep the appointment. The governor-elect of Massachusetts was told first of all that Hopkins was busy. Curley sat down and waited. In a few minutes Senator Robert M. La Follette and his brother Philip (the governor-elect of Wisconsin) came in and immediately saw the federal relief administrator. Finally Curley was told he could see Jacob Baker, a Hopkins aide, who told Curley to go back to Massachusetts and consult the regional WPA administrator about his problem. Curley was so angry that he told Baker if he could not grant the governor of Massachusetts a hearing, every wire service in the Bay State would hear about it. Hopkins's assistant then agreed to discuss some work relief proposals with the irate Bostonian, but nothing ever came of it. As Curley described the results of the conference, "It was the first of a long series of Washington 'run-arounds.' "[17]

The decision of Franklin D. Roosevelt to isolate Curley, to cut him off completely from patronage and refuse to endorse him for any political office, was the death knell for the Massachusetts governor. Curley ran for four major offices during the next seven years and was defeated each time. Roosevelt was so successful in injuring his enemy because he used a strategy of attrition rather than invasion. By breaking off communications between Curley and the White House, and by refusing to supply money or jobs, he allowed the colorful Irishman to wither on the vine.

A more aggressive strategy might well have backfired on the president. Indeed, each time Roosevelt tried to defeat a Democrat he was on the outs with, by overtly intervening in a campaign, publicly criticizing the candidate, or endorsing his enemy's opponent, he was abysmally unsuccessful. In 1938, for example, Roosevelt attempted to unseat three Democratic senators who were opposing New Deal legislation. He intervened in Georgia, South Carolina, and Maryland, going into those states and appealing to the voters to defeat Walter F. George, Ellison D. (Cotton Ed) Smith, and Millard Tydings, respectively. In each instance the president had his nose bloodied. In Massachusetts, on the other hand, Roosevelt never angered the citizens by intervening

in their local contests. Many Bay State citizens were unaware
of the president's personal feelings regarding Curley. But all the
while he was quietly pulling the rug out from under him.

Despite failure to win White House support, Curley continued
to fight for political power. In 1936 he decided to run for the
Senate rather than seek re-election as governor. Not surprisingly,
the colorful Irishman demonstrated some clout. During his two-
year term as governor, Curley tried to build a statewide organization by appointing loyal followers to state jobs and offices. On
occasion it was charged that he appointed political friends with
little thought of their qualifications.[18] Also, the audacious
governor unabashedly attached himself to Roosevelt's bandwagon. He had, for example, a newspaper-sized flyer printed and
circulated for his campaign. It carried a large photograph of himself and Roosevelt standing together arm-in-arm. The photo
carried bold-faced captions: THE NEW DEAL EXPRESS: CURLEY
AND ROOSEVELT CARRY THE NEW DEAL TO MASSACHUSETTS.
In smaller print, beneath the two smiling faces in the picture,
the flyer read: "Standing shoulder to shoulder in the same fight,
thinking mind to mind on the same policies, James M. Curley
is the choice of his close friend, President Franklin D. Roosevelt,
to promulgate the policies of the New Deal in Massachusetts. . . ."[19]

It failed to bother Curley's sense of fair play to omit that the
photograph was taken before Roosevelt became president of the
United States, and that it would be virtually impossible to get
the president to pose for such a picture in 1936. It did not bother
Curley either that to say "Curley is the choice of his close friend
. . . Roosevelt" was a compounded lie. On the contrary, the Bay
State governor had the unmitigated gall to send the president,
of all people, a different piece of campaign literature, in January
of 1936, which showed how blatantly he intended to attach himself to Roosevelt's coattails. This leaflet was headed with the
words "The Incontrovertible Record of the Democratic Party—
under—President Franklin D. Roosevelt and Governor James M.
Curley." After listing federal expenditures in Massachusetts for
house loans, buildings, industries, and welfare relief, it concluded
with the plea: "Vote the entire Democratic ticket, and let Human-
ity's Champions finish the job."[20]

Curley managed to win the senatorial nomination in 1936, but he failed miserably in the November election. James Roosevelt campaigned for Curley once again, but the president refused even to endorse him. The Walsh organization turned out the vote for their gubernatorial nominee Charles Hurley, as well as for the president of the United States, but they refused to take their coats off and work for Curley. Consequently, Hurley won and Roosevelt carried Massachusetts. Henry Cabot Lodge, Jr., defeated Curley by over 100,000 votes.

The fighting Irishman was now out in the cold. He had no public office and no patronage or money at his disposal. But, forever the optimist, James Michael Curley turned on the charm, made numerous public appearances and entered the fray to win back the mayor's seat which he had held from 1914 to 1918, and again from 1930 to 1934. His most formidable opponent was a state legislator, Maurice Tobin. A son of Irish immigrants, Tobin was a charismatic speaker who had the backing of the Walsh-Ely faction. Curley pulled all the stops, once again attempting to identify with Roosevelt to attract the president's ardent following. In this campaign Curley adopted a Roosevelt tactic he had not tried before—the fireside chat. He sent printed invitations to citizens all over Boston, inviting different groups to one of a series at the Copley Plaza Hotel.[21]

Again the Roosevelt coattail scheme failed to carry Curley through. Tobin defeated the ex-mayor by over 25,000 votes. But amazingly enough, Curley still refused to give up. He wanted to run for public office again. Almost immediately after his second scorching defeat, he was back on the campaign trail and seeking ways to get into the public eye. A case in point came in summer, 1938. Curley was out of office and had been humiliated only a few months before in the mayoralty contest. The city of Boston sponsored a swim meet. And who donated the trophy? None other than the Honorable James Michael Curley.[22]

The office Curley was after in 1938 was the governorship, presently held by his earlier rival, Charles Hurley. The never-say-die Bostonian had some reason to believe he could reverse the trend of defeats in the primary because of a split in the Walsh-Ely faction. Curley obviously could not expect the Walsh-Ely men to back him, but they were unable to agree on a candidate themselves. Hurley was running for reelection but his lieutenant-governor,

Francis R. Kelly, had his eye on the top post too. Inasmuch as the regular organization was split over Hurley and Kelly, it seemed propitious for Curley. He could enter the primary, rely on his loyal personal followers, and take advantage of the party split.

.This is precisely what Curley did. With the regular organization torn between two candidates, Curley won the primary. But several factors conspired to thwart his gubernatorial ambitions. First of all, both Kelly and Hurley organized a sizable segment of the regular organization against Curley in the general election. With the aid of ex-Governor Ely, they openly supported the Republican nominee, Leverett Saltonstall.[23] Adding to Curley's woes was the decision of a Boston judge in early 1938 that Curley had accepted approximately $40,000 while mayor, to settle a damage suit against the city in favor of the General Equipment Corporation.[24] Although Curley denied the charge and immediately appealed the case, the decision was a monstrous handicap.

Nevertheless, he refused to withdraw. He campaigned long and diligently, and once again decided to make use of the New Deal. This time he dropped the photograph of himself with Roosevelt, and he cut out the fireside chat routine. Too many people realized by 1938 that Roosevelt was not Curley's friend. Moreover, the glamour of the president and the New Deal was wearing thin now. To be sure, Roosevelt was still popular in Massachusetts, but he was no longer the demigod who could do no wrong. This was especially true by late 1938, after nearly 25,000 workers had been dropped from the WPA rolls to cut federal spending. Even though the cuts were national in scope, local citizens tended to see them as most severe in their own communities. And it was Roosevelt, of course, whom they blamed for the retrenchment policy.[25]

Consequently, Curley, who had made a habit of criticizing Washington every time there was a cut in federal funds for WPA in Massachusetts, now came out as the friend of the WPA employees.[26] His photograph appeared on the front page along with such headlines as "WPA Workers Will Support Jim Curley 100%." Curley also tried to make capital out of dissatisfaction with WPA work schedules by implying that he had convinced Harry Hopkins to increase the work week of every WPA employee by one day per week.[27]

But the new campaign strategy was not enough. Roosevelt's refusal to endorse Curley (indeed no one in Washington endorsed him), plus the regular Democratic organization's desertion to the Republican camp, were too much for Curley. Leverett Saltonstall defeated him by a 150,000-vote margin.

To the dismay of professional politicians and laymen alike, the scrapper from Boston was still around after his third drubbing in a row. His political obituary had been written by every journalist in the state, but Curley refused to read them. He confidently entered the race for mayor in 1940 hoping to unseat incumbent Maurice Tobin.

The WPA rolls were much heavier than they had been in 1938,[28] and with the imminence of war on the minds of many, Roosevelt's popularity was climbing upward. Curley again decided to try to ride the president's coattails. Just before Christmas in 1939 Curley made a trip to Washington, D. C. He managed to get a brief visit with the president, and then used it to political advantage. The *Boston American* reported that "President Roosevelt and former Governor Curley have smoked the pipe of peace. . . . The Great Estrangement is ended—definitely." The president's comment after reading the news article was, "That story about Jim Curley and me is a scream."[29]

The real scream must have been the one raised by Curley when Maurice Tobin won the right to return to the mayor's office in the city election a few months later. The voters handed Curley his fourth successive defeat. To make matters even worse, soon after the election the Supreme Court upheld the lower court's decision to make Curley pay over $40,000 to the city of Boston— money he denied he took to settle that claim in favor of a corporation.[30]

After 1940 Curley's enthusiasm for Massachusetts politics faded for a while. Indeed, he did not seek public office for two years. Then in 1942 he sought and won a seat in the United States House of Representatives. It is not surprising that the man from Boston who had organized the first Roosevelt-for-President Club over a decade before, and in return got only an offer to become minister to Poland, would take great delight in attacking President Roosevelt from the floor of Congress. In early 1943, a month after taking office, Congressman Curley launched into the president for not sending supplies into China to help those people in their struggle against Japan. A bit miffed by the attack, Roosevelt dashed off a letter to Curley. "I have read what you said in Congress and while 'the intintion is good, the ixecution [*sic*] is bum.' If I had been in Congress on the floor at that moment," the president snapped, "I would have floored you by asking you to tell me exactly how you would get additional supplies to China right away. You could not have answered that because no one else can." Curley was always as sarcastic as he was sanguine. He replied to Roosevelt, "We are living in the age of miracles and I consider you the Miracleman of the age." Curley certainly had a self-satisfied smile on his face when he went on to write, "I likewise, sometimes believe that I am a miracle-worker myself, having arisen from the dead after being interred four times and returning. . . ."[31]

Roosevelt could be a vengeful man when he wanted to be, especially if he felt it would not hurt him politically. It was not the long arm of coincidence that brought the wrath of federal investigators down on Congressman Curley within a few weeks. In early 1943 the Truman Committee investigated the Engineers' Group, Incorporated, a company which purported to be made up of experienced consulting engineers who could get war contracts for other companies. It turned out that the company was headed by a confidence man who had no pull with government agencies.

Before Pearl Harbor Curley had agreed to lend his name to the company. However, he pulled out shortly thereafter when he smelled foul play. After Curley appeared before the Truman Committee, it was obvious to Truman that he had done nothing wrong, had signed no papers, and had received no compensation. But the U. S. assistant attorney general pressed for an indictment. By September Curley had been indicted.

Not only Harry Truman was convinced of Curley's innocence; so was Senator David Walsh—and he announced his conviction publicly. Congressman John McCormack from Massachusetts tried to intercede for Curley with Roosevelt, but was told to stay out of the issue. Curley recalled in his autobiography that "by this time I was satisfied he [Roosevelt], and he alone, was responsible for framing me."[32] The last words he ever spoke or wrote to the president were, "You are nearer to being a dictator than any other man who has ever filled the office of President."[33]

The case was in federal court when Roosevelt died, and went to jury in January 1946. Despite the fact that there was not one piece of concrete evidence against Curley, he was found guilty of using the mails to defraud and sentenced to six to eighteen months in federal prison. The chief analyst of the Administration Office, United States Courts, and professor of law at Columbia University, later wrote that "few lawyers will doubt that former Mayor Curley was prosecuted for political reasons and unfairly convicted."[34]

Plenty of other people held the same view—among them President Harry S. Truman. After serving five months in prison, Curley was *pardoned,* not paroled, by Truman. As a writer for the *Nation* summed it up:[35]

... it is not every prisoner who has the minority whip of the House of Representatives circulating petitions in his behalf. Still fewer have a champion in the Cabinet, as Curley did in the person of Robert Hannegan, recently resigned. And no jailbird we ever heard of had the mayoralty of a great city held open for him while he served his time. By commuting Curley's sentence to five months, President Truman not only assured the venerable mayor of a Thanksgiving dinner at home, a touching sentiment in itself, but left intact his civil rights.

There is a great deal of irony in the Curley-Roosevelt story. The jovial Irishman, as mayor of Boston in 1931, decided in a most calculating way to attach his political future to Governor Franklin D. Roosevelt. The New Yorker's star rose rapidly, precisely as Curley gambled that it would. But Roosevelt's successes were never shared by Curley. On the contrary, the rewards he reaped were snubs from the president, a long series of defeats at the polls, and ultimately federal imprisonment. The fighting Massachusetts politician finally found victories in the congressional elections of 1942 and 1944—after he openly broke with the president. And he only found his way full circle back to the mayor's office, where it all began, after Roosevelt wanted him destroyed in 1945.

3

"WE MAY HAVE TO BE FOR ROOSEVELT WHETHER WE LIKE IT OR NOT"

EDWARD CRUMP

Anticipating the Democratic National Convention in 1944, the Tennessee senior senator, Kenneth McKellar, wrote a note to President Roosevelt about Edward H. Crump and the Tennessee Democratic organization. "He [Crump] is one of your tried and true friends from 1931–32 to date, who has always upheld and supported you. You have never had to bother about Tennessee and you will not have to do so this time."[1] McKellar was a cagey, old-line conservative, but his letters reveal him to be remarkably candid. His observation here quite accurately sums up the Crump-Roosevelt relationship. For over a decade the Memphis boss was faithful to Roosevelt, and the president and his staff in turn were loyal to Crump.

In almost every imaginable way Roosevelt's political alliance with Crump was ideal. Two or three minor disagreements notwithstanding, Crump was the kind of city boss every president must dream about. Crump promised to deliver votes at convention and election time—and he did so. The leader of the Memphis and Shelby County machine never made unreasonable, impolitic, or unethical demands on the Washington administration. He did favors for Roosevelt and only asked for his fair share of patronage in return. This was unlike the other bosses. Curley made promises but never fulfilled them. Hague, Pendergast, and Kelly, on the other hand, delivered votes and convention delegates, but their support often embarrassed the Democratic standard bearer.

Journalists from big newspapers and nationally circulated magazines were always on Roosevelt's back for working with the city bosses, but they seldom chastised him for cooperation with Crump. Angry citizens from Missouri, Massachusetts, New York, New Jersey, and Illinois inundated the president with letters urging him to break off relations with the bosses in their home states, but few letters ever came from Tennessee.[2]

Contrary to being a source of embarrassment or an undependable vote getter, Edward Crump was completely reliable, and he was a man Roosevelt never had to apologize for. As outlined in chapter 1, Crump headed the powerful Memphis and Shelby County organization, which he began building in the first decade of the century. This machine was Crump's own creation. He united around himself every major interest group in the area and kept them there by providing special services, progressive government, and low taxes.

By 1930 Crump was a household word in Tennessee politics. His organization was sound enough that he could run for the United States House of Represenatives and not worry about his machine collapsing while he was in Washington, D. C. During that first term in Congress the rookie representative failed to distinguish himself, but he did observe the political scene beyond the confines of Memphis and the Volunteer State. Although he was appalled by the conservatism and inflexibility of President Hoover, Crump was markedly impressed by the innovative programs developed by Governor Roosevelt in New York.

Consequently, by fall 1931 Congressman Crump was already on the Roosevelt bandwagon. Nearly a year before the Democratic National Convention, Crump publicly endorsed the New Yorker. "Gov. Roosevelt," he told newsmen, "has made a good governor. . . . In fact he has filled every position he has ever occupied with honor, credit, dignity, and ability. Any man who has the nerve to conquer the disease with which Gov. Roosevelt was afflicted must certainly have the stamina to wrest this country from the Republican depression."[3]

With that statement Crump became one of the first Roosevelt backers. He found it comfortable, too, because he stayed there for fourteen years until Roosevelt's death. In almost every measurable way Roosevelt was Crump's kind of man. Indeed, the two men were strikingly alike in a number of respects. Crump's biographer noted some of the similarities when he said that "both were of the aristocracy of their particular regions, yet both came to be thought of as the benefactor of the 'little' man."[4] Even more important than this, though, was the progressivism of both men. Crump, like Roosevelt, believed in the capitalist system. A capitalist himself, Crump owned a large insurance company in Memphis, as well as a great deal of property in and around the city. All the while hoping to conserve the system, Crump, like Roosevelt, believed it needed reforming. The purchasing power of the masses had to be increased. If that necessitated government spending, then so be it.

Crump not only agreed with Roosevelt that big government was necessary to preserve the system, he believed it was only right to push for it. The southern leader had a blithe spirit, contagious smile, and captivating voice. He possessed, in a word, what the future president had—charisma.

Given the similarity of their styles, it is no wonder that Crump venerated Roosevelt from the beginning. Even before the 1932 convention, when it was by no means certain that Roosevelt would win the nomination, Crump was asked whom he would put his organization behind if the governor of New York could not win. "I never make a second choice," retorted the confident Congressman; "I am for Franklin D. Roosevelt."[5]

James M. Curley exuded equal confidence and enthusiasm, but unlike Crump he failed to deliver when the votes were counted. Curley had no city or county machine to start into action, whereas Crump had one which was well oiled down to the precinct level. Crump not only controlled a dependable machine in the most populous section of Tennessee, he was on good terms with the leader of the state organization, Senator Kenneth McKellar. Whereas Curley was isolated from the state Democratic machinery, Crump had been a friend and ally of McKellar's since 1910.

The result of the Crump-McKellar alliance was that all of Tennessee's twenty-four votes went to Roosevelt on the first ballot. It was Crump's first promise to Roosevelt, and he delivered 100 percent. The Memphis boss threw his organization into action in November. He not only returned himself to Congress by a comfortable margin, but delivered Roosevelt a whopping six-to-one victory over Hoover in Memphis and Shelby County. This was notably more impressive than the overall two-to-one margin Roosevelt received in Tennessee at large.

Crump's habit of falling in behind Roosevelt carried over into the Seventy-third Congress. Literally every piece of legislation which came before the House and had been endorsed by the president got Crump's vote. He was unswervingly behind the New Deal all the way—even when it hurt him at home. His support of the "Beer Bill," which provided for the sale of beer and light wines, caused static in east Tennessee, and some associates felt he made a political blunder of the first order. There was opposition to the Economy Act, too, and Crump felt pressure to vote against this bill which called for cuts in federal employees' salaries and veterans' pensions. However, the pressure was small compared to that exerted by the powerful cotton merchants in Memphis, who were adamantly against the Agricultural Adjustment Act. In each instance, though, Crump voted the New Deal line despite contrary advice and pressure.[6]

While Crump's voting record shows that he empathized with the president, in one significant way the two men were extremely different. Roosevelt obviously had unbounded ambition in politics; Crump's goals were much more limited. After two terms in the House of Representatives, Crump had had enough. The Memphis boss himself identified first and foremost with his family and city. Life in the nation's capital was an imposition upon him, and he felt lonely and isolated. Consequently, after 1934 Crump returned to his home and devoted the next few years to spending time with his family and running Memphis politics.[7] Although he refused to run for public office himself, the ex-congressman called the shots in the Memphis Democratic organization. Gradually, too, given the importance of Shelby County in population and size, Crump became, along with Kenneth McKellar, a major power in Tennessee politics. But political prowess on a statewide scale sometimes frustrated him. In 1939 he wrote a letter to Senator McKellar which laid bare some of his inner feelings.[8]

We realize it is easy to sit on the side-lines and tell how to play the game. But we have never occupied that luxurious seat. We are in the midst of every fight—driving, pushing, shoving, hitting hard—working night and day to get out the vote and raise campaign funds, and it requires constant, never-ceasing, grilling, tiring, worrying, nerve-wracking, work every hour of the day and every day in the year to obtain that end.

We got in these State fights many years ago against my better judgment —you and Frank Rice urged it. I was very foolish not to have said then "Include me out," for we could easily take care of ourselves in Memphis and Shelby County.

But Boss Crump did not say, "Include me out." He unyield-ingly directed the Democratic forces in Memphis and used his power base to influence Tennessee politics. Precisely because he was the overseer of the largest single bloc of votes in Tennessee, and because he frequently could influence the direction of Volun-teer State politics, he was able to do much for President Roose-velt after he left Congress in 1934.

For the next ten years Edward Crump energetically and un-questioningly put the power of his machine behind Roosevelt. Tennessee's votes were united behind the president at the Demo-cratic National Convention in 1936, just as they had been four years earlier. In the general election that year the president car-ried Tennessee by over two-to-one again, and Crump's own baili-wick gave FDR an astounding thirty-to-one margin over Alfred M. Landon. When Roosevelt went for an unprecedented third-term nomination in 1940, there was Ed Crump once again solidly be-hind the man he admired, regardless of the widespread sentiment against a third term.[9]

Despite the opposition to a third term and the growing dis-illusionment with the New Deal's failure to end the depression, Crump and McKellar cranked out another two-to-one victory margin for Roosevelt in Tennessee. Memphis again topped the state's performance with a margin that was nearly seven-to-one for the president.

During the decade between Crump's return to Memphis from Congress and Roosevelt's bid for a fourth term in the White House, the Memphis leader not only threw his support behind Roosevelt at national conventions and general elections, he made numerous public speeches for the chief executive. He interviewed reporters and proclaimed the virtues of Roosevelt, "The Friend of the Human Race," and the New Deal, which gave Memphis "cheaper rents for the poor" and the TVA. When Crump did not feel like talking to reporters, he sometimes sent essays to Memphis papers which lauded the president and New Deal legislative programs.[10]

If directing delegates, turning out the votes, making speeches, and writing polemical treatises were not enough, Edward Crump used his position of power to pressure his district's congressman into supporting New Deal measures which he and Senator McKellar endorsed. Walter Chandler was the man who successfully ran for Crump's seat in the United States House of Representatives in 1934. Precisely how much influence Crump had on Chandler's voting behavior is impossible to ascertain. But it is certain that Crump made his preferences known to Chandler, and urged him to try to persuade his congressional colleagues as well.[11]

Although Crump was always a loyal Roosevelt supporter, he was by no means a slave-minded lackey. A man with a mind of his own, the Memphis boss occasionally disagreed with the president and stuck to his guns. In December 1940 Roosevelt attempted to pressure Crump on the issue of the Congress of Industrial Organizations. Crump was not anti–organized labor per se. Indeed, he had been an active friend of the American Federation of Labor. But as part of his campaign to attract new industries to Memphis, Crump was adamantly opposed to the CIO. President Roosevelt attempted to temper Crump's position but had no success whatsover.[12]

Another issue on which Roosevelt failed to gain Crump's support had to do with Senator Kenneth McKellar. Not long before his death Roosevelt telegraphed the Memphis leader to come to Washington. Crump went to the capital and spent an hour with the president. It turned out that Roosevelt wanted Crump to withdraw his support from Senator McKellar, who intended to seek reelection in 1946. Roosevelt had found it increasingly difficult to enlist the senator's support for New Deal legislation. McKellar was much more conservative than he had been in the thirties, and with his seniority was quite influential. Roosevelt hoped, with Ed Crump's assistance, to dump Tennessee's senior senator. But even though Crump himself was much more liberal than McKellar, he refused to knife his old friend and ally, even for the president he so greatly admired.[13]

Perhaps one thing which made it easier for Crump to say no to Roosevelt in 1945 than it would have been even a year earlier was the race issue. Crump, McKellar, and the state organization supported Roosevelt's nomination and election in 1944, but not without serious misgivings. The growing issue of race, especially as it related to the vice presidential nomination, was one of major concern to the Tennessee leaders.

Although Crump had organized black voters in Memphis and Shelby County, provided them with annual picnics of barbecued chicken and cheap whiskey, and allotted them certain menial jobs in the government and the political organization, the Memphis politico was a typical white southern aristocrat in his attitude toward blacks. Although he would never have condoned lynchings and brutality, he certainly did not consider blacks his equal. Patronizing blacks and keeping them in their place was his style. It was good politics to allow blacks to vote, but it was bad politics to extend them equality of opportunity. Endorsing equality for blacks was more than bad politics in Crump's eyes; it was against everything held sacred by the white-dominated society of the South.

Before the Democratic National Convention in 1944, Crump showed his disgust for even the meager strides the Roosevelt Administration was making toward equality. In a letter to Senator McKellar, himself a bigot,[14] Crump wrote:[15]

The negro question is looming big in this part of the country—in fact, all over the South. You will recall our luncheon discussion in the Capitol.

The Roosevelts dug up the negro question. Now the Republicans are going them one better. In fact, billionaire John D. Rockefeller, Jr., is taking the lead on the negro question.

There was a big dinner, social equality—negroes and whites—at the Roosevelt Hotel in New York last Thursday, honoring Walter White, a negro leader. Mrs. Roosevelt and Wendell Willkie spoke, as well as two or three negroes.

If they load down the Chicago platform with repeal of Poll Tax, Anti-Lynching and endeavoring [*sic*] to erase the Jim Crowe—that will certainly be something for us to think about. . . . We may have to be for Roosevelt whether we like it or not, but I would hate to think it wise to be placed in that position.

The Democratic platform was not "loaded down" with equal-

ity planks, and despite his misgivings Crump backed Roosevelt
in his bid for a fourth-term nomination. What the riled-up southern
boss could not bring himself to do, however, was place Tennessee behind Harry Truman's nomination for vice president. Not
only did Crump and company refrain from casting ballots for
Truman, they refused to make his nomination unanimous once
he had secured it. Crump believed the South should have been
represented by the vice presidential nominee. His choice was
their own Prentice Cooper, or Alben W. Barkley of Kentucky,
William Bankhead of Alabama, Jimmy Byrnes of South Carolina,
or Sam Rayburn of Texas. That Truman was from Missouri, a
border state and ex-slave state, made no difference to Crump.
Truman turned the Tennessee boys off because of his liberal
line on the race issue.[16]

Roosevelt was frankly worried after the convention. He was
not sure if Boss Crump would deliver the usual Tennessee majority
to the Democratic Party in November. But five weeks before the
election, a friend of Crump's told the White House not to worry.
"The enclosed interview," wrote the Tennessean, "with my good
old friend, Ed Crump, should erase the question mark in any
doubter's mind as to how the electoral vote of Tennessee will be
cast next November." The clipping quoted Crump as being extremely laudatory in his praise of Roosevelt. Crump told the
supporter his organization was planning an "all-out" campaign
for the president and Truman, and that it would not be "a half-
hearted, pussyfooting fight. . . . Who wants to return to the
Hoover-Republican old days—apple selling?"[17]

Crump was a man of his word when it came to political battles.
It was not a "half-hearted" fight on his part. Thanks to the aid
of his organization, Roosevelt carried Tennessee by a three-to-two
margin and Shelby County by nearly five-to-one. It was just as
McKellar had assured the president a year before the 1944
campaign: Crump "is one of your tried and true friends. . . . You
have never had to bother about Tennessee and you will not have
to do so this time."[18]

McKeller was correct. Crump always faithfully delivered the
votes and the delegates, even though he occasionally refused to
submit to Roosevelt's pressures on issues such as the CIO or
the dumping of McKellar. That the Memphis boss was a good and

faithful servant of the president is not particularly surprising, though, when one keeps in mind how good Roosevelt and the New Deal were to Mr. Crump, the city of Memphis, and the state of Tennessee. A scholar who investigated the impact of the New Deal on the Volunteer State concluded that "Tennessee benefitted more from the New Deal than most states."[19] In addition to all the general aid it received, Tennessee also had the exceptionally beneficial Tennessee Valley Authority. In May 1933 Roosevelt signed the TVA bill, or as it was sometimes called, the Muscle Shoals bill. When he signed it, standing beside him was a smiling, bespectacled Senator Kenneth McKellar, who had been a leading supporter of the legislation. The ear-to-ear grin on the Tennessee Democrat's face not only symbolized the pride he felt in what he had accomplished for the citizens of the region, it also reflected his joy in knowing what an asset TVA would be to himself and the Democratic Party at home.

Joining McKellar in celebrating the passage of TVA was Ed Crump. The Memphis boss reveled in the boost TVA would give the Democrats in Shelby County and the state at large, and he also realized a deep sense of personal triumph. Way back in 1915 Crump had campaigned for public ownership of utilities for his city. The privately owned power company did all it could to destroy Crump's reputation by implying that he was a corrupt public official. The company successfully led a fight that year to unseat the mayor and block any moves toward public utilities.

What delighted Crump was that now with TVA, Memphis could purchase its power from the federal government at a much lower rate than that provided by the private monopoly. After twenty years, then, Ed Crump resumed his fight against the power company—a fight the company thought it had won forever. The Memphis boss devastated the private monopoly when he got eighteen Memphians to vote for buying the company's distribution facilities, to every one vote cast on the side of the company. As Crump's biographer William Miller summed it up, "There was little question but that a majority of the Memphis populace wanted TVA power. . . ."[20]

Thanks to the TVA element of Roosevelt's New Deal, Crump won a coveted personal victory and at the same time vaulted himself to the heights of public favor in Memphis. And it was soon abundantly clear that TVA was precisely what McKellar and Crump assumed it would be from the start—an outstanding asset for the Democrats throughout Tennessee. While conservatives across the nation screamed socialism, the vast majority of Tennesseans—white and black, urbane and illiterate, rich and poor—offered prayers of thanksgiving to Franklin D. Roosevelt. TVA, of course, not only brought electric power to the people of Tennessee, indeed to the citizens of a seven-state area who had never had electricity before; it brought less expensive power to those who already had the blessing. Likewise, TVA stimulated the economy of the region as thousands were put to work harnessing the water of the Tennessee River drainage basin, reclaiming land for farming, and producing nitrogen fertilizers. All in all, the general economic and social well-being of the entire region was uplifted.

The importance of TVA in Democratic politics was obvious to all concerned. A Tennessee congressman explained to Jim Farley that "the TVA has been a very great help to the Party in Tennessee. . . ." This member of the House of Representatives went on to predict an overwhelming Roosevelt victory in 1936 because of its popularity.[21] One Shelby County politico, looking forward to the off-year election in 1938, urged his colleagues in the organization to stress TVA and TVA alone—that was the key to victory. ". . . The vast majority of the people in Tennessee are not nearly so much interested in people or personalities as they are in the success of TVA and getting TVA power in their homes. . . ." Crump responded that "we all agree," and McKellar, while urging everyone not to lose sight of other issues, agreed "that TVA is our best issue. . . ."[22]

The Crump machine in Memphis, and the Crump-McKellar statewide organization, never failed to take advantage of TVA's popularity. As the machine stalwarts campaigned for Roosevelt, and even for candidates for state and local offices, they quite deliberately mentioned TVA and what it was doing for the people of Tennessee. Such statements as "McKellar Says TVA Will Spend Millions on Flood Control Here,"[23] coming out just before primary election time, were calculated to have a stimulating effect on the state machine.

Still other New Deal programs were played up by the state and local Democratic organization once it was realized how overwhelmingly popular they were. Roosevelt's farm policy was frequently referred to during campaigns because, as one Democrat phrased it, "the Agricultural Program has reflected such a large increase in the price of farm products, and has been a very great help."[24] And in addition to farm benefits, politicians were quick to point out that thanks to the Democrats, federal money was appropriated too for completion of the Great Smokey Mountain National Park.[25]

Ed Crump injected Roosevelt and the New Deal into local campaigns at least as much as any Tennessee Democrat.[26] This was an effective strategy because the New Deal, in fact, had done so much for Memphis. It was good politics to remind the citizens of Memphis and Shelby County that a federal program had built them a class A airport, and that by April 1936 nearly $500,000 had been spent by Washington to improve the public schools. New Dealers, it could be advantageously pointed out, appropriated money for slum clearance in the southern city, and sizable funds were being spent on roads and other public improvements.

Crump's machine was certainly enhanced by the influence he used to get a CCC camp established in Shelby County.[27] But nothing was as valuable in strengthening the machine as the federal patronage which came Crump's way. The Memphis boss had built an impressive organization by doing favors for interest groups, and by astutely handing out local patronage to loyal organization workers. With the New Deal, though, came federal patronage, which was rich icing for the cake. Crump saw to it that his friend and campaign manager Frank Rice was appointed to the influential position of collector of customs. Senator McKellar consulted the machine before filling key posts in the Memphis office of the Federal Housing Administration, which was considered senatorial patronage. And the Memphis organization managed to fill the lion's share of the state's allotment on the Federal Writers Project.[28]

By far the most potent block of patronage at the disposal of the Crump machine came through the Works Progress Administration (WPA) and its forerunner the Civil Works Administration. In 1936 Tennessee had nearly 45,000 persons on federal work relief. The figure dipped to approximately 30,000 in 1938, but rose to over 44,000 by 1940.[29] Senator McKellar actually controlled the Federal Emergency Relief Administration in Tennessee. This embittered the state's junior senator, George Berry, who could not get his hands on any of the patronage. Inasmuch as national FERA director Harry L. Hopkins was determined to back McKellar, whom he viewed as the state's most powerful Democrat, no one could shake loose McKellar's hold on that invaluable patronage.[30]

Edward Crump, as would be expected, was given a generous share of the patronage by his old ally McKellar. Crump himself admitted that Shelby County deserved only about one-ninth of the WPA patronage, yet he was granted one-seventh of the total. And on at least one occasion when Crump became greedy for more patronage, the senator pressured his appointee Harry Berry, the director of Tennessee's FERA, into giving Crump an additional two hundred jobs and the promise of looking for more.[31] Democratic faction leaders who perennially tried to break the McKellar-Crump hold on state politics continually charged that the senator and the Shelby County boss had control over most of the patronage. Although Crump denied the charge, McKellar admitted it in public if the opposition was referring to "the WPA, the PWA, the RFC, and other federal set-ups."[32]

Some charges were more serious than those maintaining that the McKellar-Crump machine had most of the federal patronage at its disposal. Nearly every election time there were scores of accusations. The most common charge hurled at the organization was that WPA employees were coerced into contributing money to the campaign chest and voting for the machine's candidates. Harry Hopkins had investigators in every state looking for precisely such evidence. Despite the fact that Hopkins's investigation found Tennessee's director to be ". . . conscientious and emphatic, also effective in keeping the Tennessee ERA from becoming embroiled with State and local political factions,"[33] the evidence shows that there was some political coercion.

In summer 1937, for example, Governor Gordon Browning, who had fallen out of favor with Crump and McKellar, charged that WPA workers were causing him trouble in his administration. Senator McKellar immediately informed Director Berry that "while I want you to cooperate, I do not want too much of it."

The next winter, before the campaign of 1938, McKellar urged
Berry to keep a watch for political abuses in the WPA so that
the governor could not use it against them. But regardless of
their caution, some WPA supervisors politicized the WPA.[34]

Many workers in 1938 were angered because they were told
to contribute to the organization's campaign fund and to vote
as they were instructed or lose their jobs. Some workers had
their poll taxes paid by their foremen and were told how to vote.
One woman wrote to Harry Hopkins that "they treat all colored
peoples just likes doges [sic] down here. . . . Miss Rosella Clink
told us if we didn't vote for Mr. Crump we could lose our job. . . ."[35]

There is more evidence of political coercion than the testimony
of intimidated employees. Those who were doing the pressuring
did not always cover their tracks well. On the contrary, some
supervisors and foremen could not resist the temptation to brag
about their exploits. One supervisor wrote to McKellar that he
had paid poll taxes "and made it possible for every man under
my supervision to be a qualified voter [in the primary], and each
of these men will make an affidavit they and their influence went
100% for the coalition or the McKellar ticket. . . . [This was no
easy task, he continued, because many of my men] have had
service under Gordon Browning during the World's War. . . ."[36]

The New Deal strengthened Crump's machine in Shelby County
and the McKellar-Crump state machine as well. With over a
dozen primary and general elections held during Roosevelt's
presidency, they did not lose a single major contest. The sucesses
were due in large part to the astute organization-building of
Edward Crump—a task at which he had been working since the
early 1900s. Senator McKellar helped the organization's cause
too, by lending it his prodigious prestige and giving it his federal
patronage.

Added to these assets was the New Deal. The overwhelming
popularity of Roosevelt's legislative programs—especially TVA—
bolstered the machine politicians as they did their utmost to
identify their candiates with the New Deal. Equally instrumental
in the machine victories were the thousands of CWA and WPA
jobs under its control. On one occasion Roosevelt used his personal prestige to aid the machine even further. During the 1938
primary campaign the president was scheduled to speak in Nash-

ville. However, Nashville was the home ground of Gordon Browning, who was leading the anti–Crump-McKellar faction in a hard-fought primary. At the last minute, to aid his dedicated allies from Shelby County, Roosevelt changed locations and delivered the speech at Memphis, thus allowing Crump and McKellar rather than Browning to preside at the outstanding function. [37]

Jim Farley, postmaster general and chairman of the Democratic National Committee, also came to the assistance of Crump and company. Farley, next to Roosevelt, was probably the most influential New Dealer. In 1934 he went to Memphis and delivered a speech for the entire Democratic ticket. Then in 1940 he intervened in the state's Democratic primary—again on the side of the machine which had been behind Roosevelt since before the national convention in 1932. [38]

In the final analysis, Roosevelt and his army of New Dealers did all that they could to bolster the machine of Crump and McKellar as long as it was politically profitable. Roosevelt's actions were by no means based on any sense of loyalty to men who had thrown their support to him in 1932—his effort to pull the rug out from under McKellar before the 1946 election makes this blatantly clear. The president's apparent loyalty to Crump to the very end was dictated only by cold, calculating political self-interest. Crump had been with Roosevelt since 1932, and he always delivered the delegates and votes. Furthermore, he was a man of power in Tennessee. Although the jovial, charismatic Memphis boss refused to cave in to Roosevelt on the McKellar and CIO issues, he still controlled the largest bloc of votes in Tennessee, and unlike the conservative McKellar, he never tried to scuttle the president's domestic reform and preparedness programs.

4

ED FLYNN AND
FIORELLO LA GUARDIA

To millions of Americans Franklin Delano Roosevelt was a sincere, warm human being who felt a deep love for the people. Roosevelt may have loved "the people" in abstract, but when one examines his heartless, disloyal, and ultimately ruinous treatment of individuals he pretended to befriend, it makes one stop and wonder if he ever did *anything* without considering his own political self-interest.

The political machinations in New York during the New Deal era, especially in New York City, appear at first glance to be terribly complex—indeed, almost in a state of confusion. Communication seemed to be haphazard and unreliable among Democrats. Roosevelt acted concerned about local elections and issues one day and unconcerned the next. He seemed duty-bound and loyal to some supporters, and oblivious to the fate of others. But the aura of chaos and apparent complexity was an illusion (often deliberately created by Roosevelt) to confound the superficial observer. Actually, the politics of the nation's largest city during the Roosevelt years, as they relate to the nation's capital, are simple and clear. From 1932 until his death Roosevelt embraced or destroyed politicians on the basis of what would further his own ambition of winning and keeping office.

Tammany Hall, as was pointed out in chapter 1, refused to back Roosevelt at the National Convention in 1932. Intensely loyal to Al Smith, the Tammany gang left Chicago devastated and furious. Soon after the party donnybrook adjourned, Jim Farley paid a visit to Tammany Hall to make peace with the leaders. He recalled: "I had only one purpose in mind: to swing a united party behind Governor Roosevelt in his campaign for the Presidency, and knowing the importance of capturing the vote of New York State, I was determined to smoke the pipe of peace with the Tammany leaders."[1] And smoke the pipe of peace he did. The Hall's leaders shook hands with Farley, and quickly fell into line behind Roosevelt.

The ease with which Tammany forgot the confrontation at the National Convention was not surprising. Farley was a persuasive man who believed in party loyalty. Although he was never one to dodge a primary or convention fight, he still believed that once the blood had been spilled, everyone should make amends and put out 100 percent for the Democratic Party. The Democratic Party—*semper fidelis*—the round-faced Irishman frequently brought prodigal politicians back into line with this appeal.

The Tammanyites were ripe for Farley's party-loyalty pep talk because the Tiger lair had been losing its powerful grip on New York City since Charles Murphy died in the mid-1920s. The loss of Murphy's leadership and the stench of scandals, combined with the reduction of foreign immigration to a trickle, all combined to weaken the machine that seemed omnipotent in the old days. Consequently, the Hall was ready to forget the Roosevelt steamroller which crushed their man Smith on that hot night in Chicago. Smith was no longer in a position to do any favors for the organization, and why alienate the next president of the United States? The weakened Tiger could use all the federal patronage, money, and favors it could get. Tammany, therefore, pulled all the stops for Roosevelt in November. Everyone, for the moment at least, agreed that the bloodletting at Chicago should be forgotten.

But once Roosevelt was elected and safely tucked into the White House, he moved to cripple the Tammany organization. As soon as the New York vote had been delivered, the president viewed the organization as a potential liability. After all, beginning in 1932 with the Seabury investigations, graft and corruption had marked the machine. Also, John P. O'Brien, a Curry

man who had been elected to replace Mayor Jimmie Walker
(Walker resigned in the face of investigation), had served unim-
pressively for nearly a year. Although he was honest and hard-
working, O'Brien put his foot in his mouth every time he spoke,
and he did a miserable job of dealing with the city's problems.[2]

Consequently, when John Curry had O'Brien renominated
for mayor in 1933, despite Flynn's opposition and warning that
O'Brien could not win, Roosevelt decided to step in. Roosevelt's
reasoning, so he told Flynn, was this. Why stand idly by and watch
the Democratic Party lose control of New York City when another
Democrat could be placed in the race with a better chance of
winning? Likewise, wouldn't it be better to have a Bronx Democrat, one loyal to Flynn and himself, rather than a man like
O'Brien whose primary debt was to John Curry?

In the September 1933 election the Democrats nominated
O'Brien, and the Republican-Fusion voters nominated Fiorello
H. La Guardia. The next day Roosevelt called Flynn and asked
him to the White House for a conference. During the meeting
the president told Flynn "he was very much upset about what
was happening in Tammany Hall, and that he had been considerably distressed by the administration of O'Brien." He then re-
quested Flynn to urge Joseph V. McKee, a highly respected and
well-known Democrat from the Bronx, to enter the race on a
third-party ticket.[3]

Flynn talked to McKee, who already had been approached by
other Democrats disaffected by Tammany Hall's candidate, and
informed him of Roosevelt's wishes. After pondering the question and being assured that Roosevelt would endorse him publicly,
McKee agreed to enter the race. A new third party, the Recovery
Party, was put into the field and headed by McKee. As the three-
cornered race entered full swing, Flynn asked the president to
follow up his promise and endorse McKee. Roosevelt, however,
played a waiting game. Then, just ten days before the election,
La Guardia resorted to demagoguery and accused McKee of
anti-Semitism. Using an article McKee wrote for the *Catholic
World* in 1915, La Guardia lifted a statement from it in which
McKee had said many of the criminals in New York City were
Jewish. Out of context, the statement certainly smacked of
anti-Semitism. Whether or not McKee was actually anti-Semitic

is impossible to say. What is important to understand here is that
McKee was now in serious trouble and more than ever needed
Roosevelt's public endorsement. But despite his promise, Roose-
velt refused to act.[4]

What exactly were Roosevelt's reasons for bringing McKee
into the election? Arthur Mann, in a first-rate study of the 1933
election, argues that Roosevelt actually wanted McKee to win in
order to prevent a Republican victory and keep the city out of
the hands of the disloyal and corrupt Tammany organization.[5]
This may have been his original hope, but given his refusal to
endorse McKee—indeed, he continually denied he was behind the
Bronx Democrat[6] —and the fact that quite soon after the city
election he became extremely close to La Guardia, suggests something else. The evidence can be read to show that Roosevelt
wanted O'Brien defeated, first and foremost. If McKee should
win, that was certainly better than having a potentially disloyal
and apparently corrupt machine in power. On the other hand,
if having McKee and the Recovery Party thrown into the race
should split the Democratic vote, and leave La Guardia the victor,
that was ideal.

If we keep these few points in mind, it is not difficult to believe that Roosevelt was behind La Guardia all the time but
dared not be open about it.[7] Roosevelt never hesitated to use
people for his own benefit. Through Farley he used Tammany
Hall to get elected in November 1932, but then attacked the
organization by luring McKee into the municipal contest the
following year. Next, Roosevelt through Flynn assured McKee
he would endorse him, but never fulfilled the promise. Finally,
Roosevelt knew and liked La Guardia before the 1933 campaign.
Indeed, the Little Flower campaigned for Roosevelt in 1932.
Also, it was La Guardia who presented New Deal legislation
proposals to Congress during the months between Roosevelt's
election and inauguration.

La Guardia, defeated for reelection to the House of Representatives in the 1932 Democratic landslide, was a New Dealer in all
but party label. In the winter of 1932 Professor A. A. Berle, Jr.,
a Roosevelt Brain Truster, met La Guardia through a former
student. The mutual trust and admiration was immediate. Consequently, and with the president-elect's blessings, Berle helped

La Guardia draft bills which would get the recovery program started even before Roosevelt was sworn into office.[8]

When the rotund, five-foot-two-inch ex-congressman returned to New York City in March of 1933, he carried with him an impressive national reputation as a fighter for liberal legislation. As Arthur Mann, La Guardia's biographer, noted, "Roosevelt agreed that the East Harlem Republican was one of them emotionally and ideologically."[9] The other factor which endeared La Guardia to Roosevelt was his popularity. The Little Flower was of both Italian and Jewish descent, he was a practicing Episcopalian, and his wife was a German Lutheran. A multilingual, charismatic, energetic, and magnetic fellow, La Guardia was a politician's politician, with outstanding credentials for popularity in New York. As the mayoralty campaign progressed, the *Literary Digest* continually and accurately predicted that the Manhattan Messiah would win.

No wonder, then, that President Roosevelt refused publicly to endorse McKee. Why alienate La Guardia, a potentially valuable long-term ally? The Little Flower, after all, was a New Dealer at heart; his political future as a Republican was dim; and he was, above all, popular. Roosevelt could not, however, openly endorse La Guardia, for that would alienate too many loyal Democrats.[10] His hands-off policy, once he got McKee in the race, was politically the most prudent course to follow.

At first Roosevelt's long-range strategy in New York was not apparent. Jim Farley and Ed Flynn had plans, and for some time they assumed Roosevelt shared them. Farley and Flynn hoped to take control of the Democratic Party machinery in New York, and ultimately of Tammany Hall itself. Both these men were party regulars, and it never occurred to them to do anything but build a strong Democratic machine with loyal party regulars.

Flynn already had a solid organization in the Bronx as a base of operations. Paradoxically, after the Democrats were defeated by La Guardia in 1933, Flynn's machine grew even stronger. The Bronx boss remembered that[11]

... the Democratic party in the Bronx emerged in a stronger position than any other Democratic organization in the city. We protected our local candidates and preserved the local patronage that came from their offices.

Blessed with good relations with the White House and the Executive Mansion in Albany, we were in a better position to survive the La Guardia regime than any other New York City political group.

Flynn's strong position among Democrats in New York City, plus the close ties both he and Farley had with the new governor, Herbert Lehman (Lehman had been Roosevelt's lieutenant governor, and Roosevelt, Flynn, and Farley had hand-picked him over Tammany's opposition to be the party's gubernatorial nominee in 1932), made them confident that a new Democratic machine could be forged to run the city and state.

Farley became chairman of the state Democratic Committee and Lehman controlled the state funds and patronage. With help from Washington, Flynn would be able to wrest control of Tammany from Curry. Then the Democratic Party under the aegis of Flynn and Farley could run the political affairs of the nation's largest city and state.

Soon after Fiorello La Guardia was sworn in as mayor of New York, it became obvious to insiders in New York politics that President Roosevelt had his own plans for the city, and they did not harmonize with those of his closest political advisors, Farley, Flynn, and Howe. The president felt no loyalty to party per se.[12] He intended to stay in power, and he would use any means at his disposal to do so. Roosevelt did not want Flynn and Farley to assume the leadership of Tammany Hall—he wanted the Hall destroyed. Part of the reason was personal. Upon entering New York state politics, young Roosevelt was nearly broken by Tammany's forces, and was forced to compromise with them to survive. Although he sought and received the Hall's support when he ran for governor, he remembered well how it nearly prevented him from getting the presidential nomination in 1932.

Beyond these personal grudges, Roosevelt had two other important reasons for attacking the Tiger. First of all, the scandals of the Walker regime had turned a large share of public opinion sour on the machine. The stench was nearly as bad as the one which permeated New York during the halcyon days of the Tweed Ring. Second, there was a captivating, dynamic new leader in Manhattan, and his name was Fiorello La Guardia.

As Roosevelt could see, the Manhattan Messiah had achieved

political prominence in New York and planned to keep it. Ed
Flynn observed that La Guardia was, next to Smith and Roosevelt
himself, "the smartest politician I have ever met in my political
career."[13] Certainly, Roosevelt had recognized the Little Flower's
political sagacity as well. Not only was La Guardia smart, he
was a determined character with monumental ambition. Because
Tammany's leaders got caught with their hands in the taxpayers'
cookie jar in 1932, many people were ready for a new regime.
La Guardia established it by putting together a coalition of ethnic
minorities, native liberals, and Republicans who were not terribly
concerned about his unorthodoxy. And because La Guardia was
such a shrewd politician, he had built, and would continue to
nurture, a solid machine. He was not at all as naive as many of
the so-called reformers who came to power occasionally after a
political scandal but quickly lost their holds on the administration
because they refused to construct an organization. Not La Guardia.
He was no idealist. He could use the reform rhetoric with the
best of them, but he was cut out of the boss tradition. He knew
that a machine was essential to winning and *keeping* office.[14]

Roosevelt, then, had very little to gain by attempting to bury
the hatchet with Tammany, or even by helping Flynn and Farley
assume command. Tammany Hall was hardly riding on a crest
of popularity in the early thirties. La Guardia, on the other hand,
was extremely popular. Because New York's new mayor also
shared his political philosophy, why should not the president
cultivate La Guardia's support and dump his old enemies at
Tammany Hall?

Roosevelt's strategy quickly took shape. He would support
Flynn's existing organization in the Bronx, solidify a Democratic
state organization around his own men, and then do all in his
power to help La Guardia establish himself as the boss of New
York City. The La Guardia dimension of this strategy was, of
course, anathema to Flynn and Farley. They believed in party
loyalty and found the chain of command of Democratic organizations from the local to the national level functional and effective.
These two stalwarts continually tried to discourage the president
from aiding the Little Flower. And when they failed, they
deeply resented Roosevelt and viewed him as a traitor to his own
party.[15]

The La Guardia arm of the president's New York strategy
was eminently successful. Tammany Hall, weakened by the
Walker administration scandals and then isolated by Roosevelt's
master plan, failed to revive in any way approaching its earlier power
and glory until after World War II. The Democrats could not
elect a mayor in New York City until La Guardia voluntarily
retired in 1945. Richard Polenberg accurately described the
demise of Tammany Hall: [16]

During the 1930s, as Tammany Hall's political power waned, New York
City Democrats bewailed the reversal of fortune suffered by their once-
powerful machine. By 1938, Jeremiah T. Mahoney, who had been the Democratic candidate for mayor a year earlier, reported: "Things in our local
Democratic organization are at the lowest ebb, and nobody seems to care
much whether local organization progresses or dies." In the spring of 1939,
Mahoney observed, the situation had not improved: "Tammany Hall is still
plodding along at the bottom of the sewer. Nobody is doing anything to revive our old organization."

The Hall's failures were partly due to urban changes which
were discussed in detail in the last chapter. But it would be naive
to discount the monumental impact of the Roosevelt–La Guardia
alliance. Of course, La Guardia, who was gifted with an unusually
generous share of sagacity and charisma, helped his own cause
immensely. He not only put together a city-wide organization
based on his doing favors and providing jobs, he kept the citizens
turned on by his continual antics. Bouncing and bursting with
energy, the pudgy little mayor—a perfect subject for caricature—
was always doing something to make headlines. His contemporary
Robert Moses listed some of the performances which made him
absolutely remarkable and unforgettable: [17]

. . . rushing to fires, reading the comics, leading the band, helping Grover
Whalen to greet trained seals fresh from swimming the English Channel,
jeering at stuffy tycoons knee-deep in soft rugs in Park and Fifth Avenue clubs
or at "tinhorns" in the less elegant bistros, crucifying a market inspector for
accepting a cheap necktie from a pushcart peddler, acting as a committing
magistrate to pillory a welfare inspector who did a favor for somebody on
relief . . . firing a faithful, if sometimes sappy secretary for getting tight,
driving the gay hurdy-gurdies from the streets, screaming obscenities at
Mussolini's Virginio Gayda over the Italian trans-Atlantic radio, denouncing

the Greyhound bus official as "Grey Muts" . . . berating offending City
Hall reporters, taking away policemen's clubs, directing traffic, laying out
airports, acting as impresario of the City Center, proposing with impish
glee to hang the wet wash in the back of Gracie Mansion where everyone in
Carl Shurz Park could see the short and simple flannels of the ruling family,
and beating his breast and quoting Timothy that he had fought a good
fight and kept the faith.

    Showman La Guardia had many qualities similar to those of
Theodore Roosevelt. As a matter of fact, it is tempting to believe
he must have idolized the Republican Roosevelt and done his
best to imitate him. Both were boastful, proud of their war
records, and eager to reenter the military after political careers.
Both men were ham actors who frequently went to great lengths
to win public recognition. Both used the rhetoric of reform but
built machines which were the envy of every boss in the nation.
And both, while officially Republicans, were hardly devotedly
"regular."

    If La Guardia studied the political style of the Roosevelt he
looked so much like, he must have noted that charisma alone
could not bring victory. Theodore Roosevelt's machine fell apart
after he left the White House in 1909, and he was unable to win
reelection after four years absence. La Guardia sustained himself
in city hall through 1945 by diligently laboring to keep his machine
intact.

    Perhaps La Guardia could have won and kept office from
1932 to 1945 without the blessing of Franklin D. Roosevelt—but
it is highly improbable. Roosevelt injected McKee into the mayoralty election in 1933 and thereby assured La Guardia's victory.
Moreover, if Roosevelt had followed the wishes of Farley and
Flynn, he no doubt could have channeled federal patronage,
money, and favors in such a way as firmly to reestablish Tammany
Hall under his own aegis.

    There is no question that the president's determination to
help La Guardia was the major impetus behind the prodigious
growth of a new machine in New York City. White House support
for La Guardia came in several packages, but the largest and most
valuable was control of federal work relief programs. The extent
of Roosevelt's commitment to La Guardia can be seen in the
unique way New York was handled. Forty-seven of the nation's

forty-eight states had a director of federal work relief programs appointed by Harry Hopkins. As national director of the FERA, Hopkins asked the senators of each state to recommend a director—that is, the senators of each state with the exception of New York, where the process was more complex.

New York's Democratic senators recommended a Democrat, of course. And while the appointment was agreeable to Flynn and Farley, it was totally unacceptable to Mayor La Guardia. Whoever the state administrator would be, he would be in complete charge of patronage. With a loyal Democrat as administrator, La Guardia feared the patronage in the city would be used to strengthen Tammany at his expense. This is precisely what would have happened, but Roosevelt was not about to see the mayor devastated in this way.

Consequently, using the excuse that New York City was so large that it should have its own director who was independent of the New York State administrator, Roosevelt allowed La Guardia to appoint the director for the city and the senators appointed the director for the rest of the state.[18] This move not only destroyed Flynn's hopes for Tammany Hall, it gave the Independent-Republican mayor tens of thousands of building blocks for his machine. The significance of this appointment's going to Fiorello La Guardia can be appreciated only by realizing that New York City's share of the WPA expenditures was one-seventh of the total WPA expenditures for the entire nation.[19] Although the number of persons employed in federal work relief programs fluctuated sharply, by March 1936 nearly 240,000 people were on the WPA rolls in New York City.[20]

It is obvious what such an enormous patronage plum did for La Guardia's organization. With all these federal jobs added to the city positions already at the mayor's disposal, it is no wonder that Tammany Hall's power declined quite markedly during the 1930s. But if jobs alone were not sufficient to bolster the new city regime, Roosevelt did even more. He saw to it that hundreds of millions of dollars were poured into construction projects for New York City. PWA grants and loans for public projects amounted to over $250,000,000, and WPA funds rolled into the city at a rate of $145,000,000 a year until 1938.[21]

Thanks to the federal spending in New York City, which was

greater than in any other American community, La Guardia's constituents saw the construction of six hospitals, numerous health centers, Hunter College, a domestic relations court building, a seaplane terminal, half a dozen sewage plants, and a host of other public facilities. Like James Michael Curley in Boston, the Little Flower frequently pointed to these projects as contributions by his administration. Always, however, he acknowledged the Roosevelt administration as the city's benefactor.[22]

On several occasions the president personally went to New York City to "inspect" projects which were funded by federal programs. On each trip La Guardia accompanied Roosevelt as he made the rounds and addressed the grateful crowds. Roosevelt scored points for himself by making these appearances, but he also added immeasurable cubits to the mayor's stature by appearing in person with him. Roosevelt never snubbed Ed Flynn by excluding him from these political outings, but he frequently let La Guardia help plan the itineraries so that they would work to the greatest advantage of all concerned.[23]

Roosevelt did still more for La Guardia. He refused to endorse openly the incumbent for reelection in 1937, but he refused to disavow him and support the Democratic nominee. This infuriated Flynn and Farley, but they were powerless to do anything about it. When Roosevelt was questioned about the mayoralty election at a press conference in August that year, all he would say was, "I am keeping my hands off the campaign, completely and absolutely." The president was true to his word if he meant by keeping his "hands off" he would not openly endorse a candidate. As far as Farley was concerned, though, it was tantamount to supporting La Guardia when the president, a Democrat, would not endorse the regular Democratic ticket.[24]

Farley's assessment was close to the mark. It was highly irregular for Roosevelt not to say a good word for a Democratic candidate in a general election, although he *usually* avoided taking stands in primaries. And while it would have been impolitic for him to endorse the opposition, most people knew Roosevelt's sympathies were with Fiorello. It was no secret, after all, that the president had close personal ties with La Guardia. Indeed, Roosevelt had a closer relationship with the Little Flower than he had with any other city boss except Ed Flynn. Roosevelt genuinely valued the mayor's company. He respected his opinions on political matters and enjoyed his friendship as well. It was common knowledge that La Guardia and his wife, and sometimes their children, went to Hyde Park for overnight visits and summer picnics.[25]

Roosevelt had grown so close to La Guardia by the time of the 1941 city election that he endorsed him just short of saying "Vote for La Guardia." He told a press conference just before the election that he had[26]

lived and worked in the City of New York off and on since 1904. I have known and observed New York's Mayors since that time. I am not taking part in the New York City election, *but*–(laughter)–what are you all laughing at?–(more laughter)–*but,* because the City of New York contains about half the population of my State, I do not hesitate to express the opinion that Mayor La Guardia and his Administration have given to the City the most honest and, I believe, the most efficient municipal government of any within my recollection.

That night La Guardia sent him a telegram which contained only one word:[27]

Merci,

Fiorello

This little nudge from Roosevelt no doubt helped. La Guardia was reelected with ease. The organization turned out the vote for the incumbent, just as it had done for the president in 1936, and 1940, and would do again in 1944.

For nearly a decade Roosevelt had harnessed the energies of his administration and put them behind the Manhattan Messiah. He did so not just because he had grown fond of the ebullient little man who was always making headlines, but because La Guardia was one of the president's most valuable assets. To be sure, La Guardia faithfully and successfully put his organization behind Roosevelt in every election, but he did more too. As president of the National Conference of Mayors, La Guardia wielded a lot of influence in the cities of the nation. He obtained support for administration programs, and he kept his fingers on the pulse beat of urban America. His frequent contacts with mayors of cities of every size kept him abreast of issues in cities, and he was able to advise the president on subjects to hammer away at in his campaign for reelection.[28]

La Guardia also campaigned for Roosevelt in every national election. A well-known and attractive public speaker, New York's mayor stumped for the head of the Democratic ticket all over the United States. In Chicago, Cincinnati, Buffalo, Gary, Detroit, New Haven, Boston, and Philadelphia. as well as at home, La Guardia spoke on radio and in person. He added color and prestige to campaigns, and he offered the additional asset of being an "Independent" for Roosevelt who urged Republicans and the nonaligned to cross over to the Democrats.[29]

The Little Flower was especially helpful in New York in 1936 when, at Roosevelt's behest, he organized the American Labor Party. This third party was created primarily to attract liberals of every stripe, from socialist to independent Republican, to support Roosevelt. Having a third party for Roosevelt enabled those who approved of Roosevelt but who could not vote Democratic becasue of Tammany Hall to be able to cast a ballot. This third party strategy was eminently successful. Nearly 250,000 voters who could not bring themselves to vote Democratic cast their votes for Roosevelt on the ALP in New York City in 1936.[30]

The pipe-smoking, cigar-chewing little mayor often worked around the clock for Roosevelt. He surely did much of this for his own self-interest: he nevertheless was intensely loyal to the president. But despite La Guardia's intense loyalty, Franklin D. Roosevelt was able to break a promise and a heart. He decided to forsake his friend rather than do anything to jeopardize himself politically. As Rexford Tugwell phrased it, "that La Guardia was treated badly by Roosevelt . . . is a tragic reminder of practicality in politics."[31]

What happened was this. It seems that La Guardia always had his heart set on getting an appointment in Washington with the Roosevelt administration. Before this, however, he wanted to run for governor of New York, or for the Senate, but Roosevelt would not give him the green light because Farley and Flynn absolutely would not go along with it. As late as 1940, seven or eight years after the La Guardia–Roosevelt alliance was formed, Ed Flynn and Jim Farley still could not graciously accept the Little Flower. La Guardia candidly admitted he did not speak the same language Farley did.[32] Although these men were always cordial to each other, La Guardia was not a Democrat. It was just that simple.

Without the endorsement of the two most powerful Democrats in New York, La Guardia could not dream of getting the Democratic gubernatorial or senatorial nomination. The Democratic Party was his last-ditch hope because the upstate Republicans wanted no part of the radical mayor who had too many hyphenated American ideas. So, with no hope of securing a spot on either ticket as a senatorial or gubernatorial nominee, La Guardia set his sights on Washington.

The mayor felt Roosevelt owed him a position in the administration, given his extraordinary loyalty and hard work for the ticket since 1932. Roosevelt apparently got La Guardia's hopes up for being named secretary of war; he was dissatisfied with Harry Woodring, who held the post until 1940. He decided to drop Woodring and appoint a Republican because of the need for a united nation in the event of United States involvement in the war. But Roosevelt backed off on La Guardia because, as he bitterly told Tugwell, "the Democrats" (meaning, of course, Farley and Flynn) among his advisors were adamantly opposed.[33]

Henry L. Stimson was the Republican who ultimately got the nod. As a consolation prize to the saddened La Guardia, Roosevelt promised him a commission as a brigadier general just as soon as we entered the war. The Little Flower immediately perked up. The president was going to make him a general, and perhaps he would go to Italy. In his typical impetuous style, La Guardia ordered his uniform and made preparations for a military leave of absence from city hall.[34]

The months and years went by, but the commission never arrived. An ex-flyer from World War I, La Guardia grew impatient to get back in uniform. He wrote to Roosevelt early in 1943 and said, "I still believe Genl. Eisenhower can *not* get along without me and am awaiting your order."[35] By summer the excitable veteran could not contain himself. He dashed off another note to Roosevelt: "Dear Chief: Soldier La Guardia reports to the C. in C. that he awaits orders. —He believes General Eisenhower needs him now more than ever." It was signed "F. La Guardia, Major U. S. Air Service, 1st W. W."[36]

Despite the president's promise, the commission never came. Evidently General Eisenhower was not very excited, to say the least, over the prospect of having dynamo La Guardia underfoot in the midst of a war. Nevertheless, Roosevelt continued to dangle the charm until after the election of 1944. He was not about to alienate the Little Flower before the election, especially since Farley had broken with him after the third term—a development which did not do the president any good in New York State.[37]

As usual, La Guardia campaigned for the president's reelection, and he delivered his organization's vote in November 1944. After the votes were counted, the promise to the mayor was forgotten. This ego-devastating blow took much of the fight out of La Guardia. He decided against seeking reelection in 1945. Uncharacteristically for the vivacious, perpetual-motion machine, La Guardia went into retirement. He died two years later.

La Guardia was by no means the only New Yorker Franklin Roosevelt used and then discarded. Perhaps even more heartless was his treatment of Edward J. Flynn. As outlined in chapter 1, Flynn was a quiet, introspective attorney who got into politics rather by accident. An atypical Irish politician, Flynn was an intellectual who would rather read books than talk to people. After the leadership of the Bronx was more or less placed in his lap, he tightened up the Democratic organization there by astutely handing out patronage, running an efficient borough, and avoiding the scandals of graft that had plagued the Walker administration. His alliance with Roosevelt went back to 1928, when he had campaigned for him for governor. After Roosevelt won the election, he rewarded Flynn with the major post for patronage distribution in the administration, secretary of state.

From that point on Flynn became, next to Louis M. Howe, Roosevelt's closest friend and political advisor. It was Flynn who suggested bringing Farley onto the Roosevelt team. Together they engineered Roosevelt's nominations and victories of 1932 and 1936. Farley broke with the team in 1940, so Flynn alone became the architect of the third- and fourth-term nominations and elections. The third- and fourth-term campaigns will be analyzed in chapter 6, but suffice it to say here that Flynn, while remaining titular head of the Bronx organization during the 1930s and 1940s, was for all practical purposes the head of the national Democratic organization. He shared the honors with Farley until 1940. After that, until Roosevelt's death, he handled the job alone.

Samuel I. Rosenman, a member of Roosevelt's staff since 1928, summed up Flynn's inestimable value to Roosevelt this way: Roosevelt[38]

always tried to get the truth—whether good or bad—about the prospects for the national and local tickets. He did not always get the truth because there were many who liked to tell him only good news. There were some, however, on whom he could always rely for frank and accurate appraisals, no matter how brutal they might be. Edward J. Flynn, then one of the most competent and intelligent of the political leaders in the United States, was one; Ed Kelly of Chicago, Frank Walker, and James A. Farley were others.

Flynn himself recalled that the president frequently used him as "a trial balloon."[39] Before Roosevelt became president, and especially thereafter, Ed Flynn often huddled with him on political matters. Absolutely no city boss had as much access to Roosevelt. Indeed, Flynn saw the president more often than all the other city bosses combined—including La Guardia, who beat a path to the White House door.[40]

The frequent visits, the mutual respect, and the memories of numerous hard-fought battles since 1928 bound the two New York politicos together. It is probably safe to say that after Howe died in 1936, nobody was as close to Roosevelt as Flynn. The Bronx Irishman exchanged gifts with the president, and knew him well enough to pick out suits, shirts, and ties that would delight the Hyde Park aristocrat.[41]

The president exploited his friend and advisor so completely that at times he even experienced feelings of guilt. In August of 1940, with a third presidential campaign in the offing, Roosevelt sent a letter of apology to Mrs. Flynn: "Dear Helen," wrote the president,[42]

For some time I have been meaning to write to you to apologize for having taken your Ed away from his family for the next two months. I know that I need not tell you how much it means to me to know that he is running the campaign, and that I appreciate the sacrifices both of you are making. I do hope you will forgive me and also that you will come up to see me soon and let me tell you again that I am both apologetic and grateful.

Most of Flynn's labors for his chief were labors of love. The way Roosevelt used him in 1933, however, left a lasting scar. Remember that Flynn asked McKee to enter the mayoralty race at Roosevelt's behest. McKee was Flynn's personal friend. The Bronx leader was hurt and embarrassed when the president refused to endorse McKee. Apparently, he never even intended to do so.[43]

In 1938 Roosevelt ignored the advice of both Farley and Flynn by determining to "purge" some anti–New Deal Democrats in the primary elections. The president's prestige was markedly damaged when the senators he tried to oust in Georgia, South Carolina, and Maryland were renominated despite his intervention. But once again, despite the warnings of Flynn and Farley, he opted to purge another Democrat who had been crippling his legislative proposals. This time Roosevelt's sights were set on the late summer Democratic primary in New York. His senatorial opponents had just handed him an embarrassing defeat, and now he was going to tackle John J. O'Connor, a congressman from New York City and a member of the House Rules Committee.

Roosevelt tried to get Farley to lead the primary campaign against O'Connor. Farley flatly refused. He said he did not want to take part in this kind of battle in New York, and besides, he believed the difficulties between O'Connor and the president could be ironed out.[44] Realizing Flynn felt the same way, Roosevelt prompted Tom Corcoran to try purging him. But it was soon obvious that Corcoran—the rankest sort of amateur at the game of politics—was botching up the campaign. Therefore, in desperation Roosevelt called Flynn at Lake Tahoe in California where he was vacationing, and begged him to come back to New York and direct the campaign of James H. Fay—the man Corcoran had persuaded to run against O'Connor.[45]

Up to this point Flynn had managed to keep his hands clean of the purge. He loathed such a business. But he succumbed to Roosevelt's persuasion, and he went back and led a successful race which unseated O'Connor. Throughout the battle O'Connor screamed that the WPA was being used against him. Political coercion, he charged, was being used to get workers to vote for Fay under the threat of losing their jobs. Nothing was ever done to make amends, but the evidence clearly suggests that O'Connor's accusations were correct.[46]

Flynn deeply disliked the O'Connor purge, but he disliked O'Connor personally, so that made the distasteful business slightly easier.[47] But in the final analysis, he never would have done it if it had not been for his love for his friend, the president.

His devotion to Roosevelt was demonstrated by more than his loyal service as advisor, campaign director, and purge pilot. When Jim Farley broke with Roosevelt over the third term in 1940, Roosevelt asked Flynn to take Farley's place as chairman of the Democratic National Committee. Roosevelt was especially concerned about this post being filled by one who could be an effective liaison officer between the big city bosses and himself. Farley had worked well with the bosses. Now, with him out in a huff, the new chairman just had to be effective at that level. The logical candidate, of course, was Flynn.

The Bronx boss was not interested in the chairmanship of the national committee. He admittedly was an introvert who disliked talking to reporters and gladhanding politicians. Besides being a loner, Flynn was a devoted family man. Extremely close to his wife, Helen, he did not relish the thought of adding the national chairmanship to his duties as advisor and Bronx skipper. All these reasons had prompted Flynn to bring Farley into the circle years before, and to urge his appointment as national chairman.[48]

But the ever-loyal Flynn saw his boss in trouble once again. Roosevelt charmed and persuaded him to accept the office—but on the understanding that he would be allowed to resign immediately after the November election. Typically, Roosevelt, thinking of his self-interest rather than his associates, agreed to this plan but then put Flynn off on the resignation for nearly three years.

It is unfortunate that Roosevelt badgered his reluctant friend into the chair. His new post brought him too much publicity and public scrutiny. Those who liked the limelight would have found it attractive. Flynn, of course, found it anathema. Moreover, the heaviest cross this soft-spoken man had to bear in all of his long public life grew out of his overwork as national chairman. Soon after he took the job, his wife was landscaping a summer house they had purchased in Putnam County. Their landscape architect had difficulty finding paving stones to lay in a patio she had designed. Flynn agreed to see if he could locate materials by speaking to a political associate, the Bronx commissioner of public works. The commissioner took it upon himself to handle the paving block problem while Flynn was touring the country on national committee business. Flynn paid one bill to have the stones moved upstate from the Bronx, but thought no more about it. It turned out that the stones were laid by city employees working on public payroll time. Flynn swore he knew nothing of this until an investigation was undertaken.

Ultimately, a grand jury found him innocent. And indeed, it seems incredible to believe that Flynn, who survived the Seabury investigations as clean as a hound's tooth and refused to support those of his men involved in corruption, would risk public censure by deliberately stealing the labor costs on a project where labor and materials combined cost less than $750.[49]

After a grand jury investigation the issue was closed—or so it seemed, at least. The Bronx chairman had been exonerated, so there was little more to say. Then in late winter 1942 Roosevelt decided he wanted Ed Flynn to don a new hat. With full-scale war waging, national politics were hardly the most crucial of his problems. He therefore asked Flynn to resign as Bronx and national chairman and accept an appointment as minister to Australia and ambassador-at-large for the South Pacific. As Flynn phrased it, "I was to be his personal representative in the South Pacific."[50]

Now slightly balding, but trim and impeccably dressed, the Democrat from the Bronx gladly accepted the offer. It was an excuse to get out from the national chairmanship and find a refreshing change of scenery. Moreover, it gave him a sense of contributing more during wartime than he was doing in the Democratic Party.

To the total dismay of everyone in Roosevelt's inner circle, the Senate did not automatically rubberstamp Flynn's appointment. Instead, a number of senators who were on the outs with the president attacked the nominee as a city "boss," with all the derogatory connotations such a label bears. As part of the smear campaign the paving block episode was dragged out once again. With his reflex-like loyalty to Roosevelt, Flynn immediately withdrew his name so that the president would not have to suffer any embarrassment. And Roosevelt, with his reflex-like action or loyalty to his own political self-interest, immediately accepted Flynn's resignation as nominee.

Could not the president have stood up for his friend? Would it have been so difficult to denouce the senators and defend the character of Edward J. Flynn? To do these things, of course, would have been out of character for Franklin D. Roosevelt. He had made a habit of deserting his friends and allies if they stood in the way of his own ambitions. Formally and on the record, all that Roosevelt did in response to Flynn's resignation was to write him a letter saying, "Reluctantly, I am complying with your request and have withdrawn your nomination from the Senate. I wish you would come and see me today or tomorrow." Eleanor Roosevelt, who always had deeper feelings of personal loyalty than her husband, wrote the following letter to a saddened and depressed Edward Flynn:[51]

My Dear Ed,

I have hesitated to write to you, because I realize that the last few weeks must have been a terrible strain. You must have the satisfaction of knowing that you have done a good job and kept faith with your own convictions and ideals through these past years, so that the accusations and clamor, which are purely political, probably do not touch either you or Helen very deeply.

It is difficult to explain these things, however, to your children, and for them I feel sure you have been deeply troubled. In time they will understand, but now it must be hard. . . .

This letter . . . is only to assure you of my personal loyalty and admiration and my hope that through the years we will continue to be good friends.

Flynn, in his typical fashion, forgot the hurt and continued to be a loyal friend to both of the Roosevelts. In 1944 he once again helped direct the president's campaign. In early 1945 Roosevelt took the Bronx Democrat with him to Yalta, and then sent him on to Rome. The president was certain there could never be a permanent peace unless Roman Catholics in Russia and other eastern European countries were allowed to worship freely. Flynn, a devoted Catholic and trusted aide, was the man Roosevelt felt should work on the problem.

Flynn had just completed a series of talks on the Catholic issue when news came of the president's death. With Elliott Roosevelt, Sam Rosenman, and Bernard Baruch, he flew back to the United States for the president's funeral.

Edward J. Flynn had done all he could to ease the way for Catholics in eastern Europe, and he had performed his final service for Franklin D. Roosevelt. The long-time man of power from the Bronx gradually withdrew from national political life, although he continued to serve as chairman of the executive committee of the Bronx County Democratic organization. He died from a heart attack in 1953 while vacationing in Dublin.

5

"HE WAS WITH US FROM THE START"

THOMAS J. PENDERGAST

Thomas Joseph Pendergast, a short, round man with a bald head, sparkling dark eyes, and genuinely warm smile, met a fate similar to that of most of the city bosses who aligned themselves with Franklin D. Roosevelt. As long as he was a political asset to the president, he was showered with favors from Washington. But once it was assured that he was a political liability, Roosevelt destroyed him without blinking or flinching.

In 1933 Tom Pendergast seemed to be as firmly established in Missouri politics as the Pope was in the Roman Catholic Church. He had a dependable machine in Kansas City and rural Jackson County. The 1932 election brought victory to his hand-picked gubernatorial candidate Guy B. Park. And with Park's ascent to the governor's mansion, all the state patronage went to the machine. As a federal investigator from Washington remarked, "It is observable that through Park, Pendergast gets the state appointments. The state house is lousy with Pendergast men."[1]

Besides the state patronage, the Kansas City boss soon had complete control of nearly all federal patronage in Missouri, until by the mid-thirties he had what was probably the best organized Democratic machine in any state of the Union with the possible exception of Hague's New Jersey organization. What is incredible is that by 1938 it suddenly began to crumble; by 1939 the boss was in federal prison; and by the time of Roosevelt's third election, the Pendergast machine was only a legend.

The meteoric rise and fall of the House of Pendergast is an interesting story which cannot be understood outside of a New Deal context. Pendergast's control of Kansas City and Jackson County was seldom challenged by the time of Roosevelt's first election, but Republicans had controlled the state house throughout the twenties. The national Democratic landslide in 1932 insured a Democrat's becoming governor. That the governor would be a Pendergast man was undisputed, inasmuch as the man from Kansas City had the largest and only dependable Democratic machine in the state. His domination of the Missouri Democrats was an established fact.[2]

The depression no doubt made a Democratic victory inevitable in Missouri in 1932. This in itself would have given Pendergast control of the state patronage and purse strings. That Roosevelt, rather than Al Smith or someone else, became president had a marked effect on Pendergast's control of federal programs, and these programs extraordinarily enhanced his position of power in the Show-Me State.

It all began in 1931 when Pendergast went to New York and met with Governor Roosevelt, Jim Farley, and Ed Flynn. There he agreed to support them at the national convention the following summer. The result of Pendergast's early jump onto the Roosevelt-for-President bandwagon was the promise of federal patronage if the New York governor won the election. As was pointed out in chapter 1, Pendergast backed Roosevelt at the convention, and then put his machine into high gear during the autumn campaign.

Soon after the inauguration in 1933 the administration began dispersing the federal spoils. Jim Farley announced to the Missouri senator, Bennett Clark (a St. Louisian and not a member of Pendergast's organization), that a portion of patronage usually reserved for senators was going to Pendergast. Clark was furious, but Farley informed the senator that it had been promised to the Kansas City boss, who in Farley's words "was with us from the start."[3]

With Roosevelt's blessing Farley bent over backwards to do favors for Tom Pendergast. One of the first things he did was to intervene in the appointment of Missouri's state director of federal reemployment. It seems that Secretary of Labor Frances

Perkins appointed a Republican from the little town of Maryville to be the director. But the ink was barely dry on the secretary's selection when the appointment was withdrawn, and Pendergast's hand-picked choice, a judge from Jackson County named Harry Truman, was given the post.[4]

Farley always did his best to help Tom Pendergast. The two men got along extremely well, partly because they were so much alike. It is true that Farley never condoned graft or corruption, and he certainly deplored ballot box stuffing. But none of these offenses was proved to be part of Pendergast's modus operandi until 1939, so for years Farley never had to apologize for associating with the Missouri boss. Actually, the two men had much in common. Both were of Irish ancestry; they came from very humble beginnings and were dedicated individuals who had worked hard to pull themselves up by their own bootstraps. Lifelong Democrats, each believed in party discipline and loyalty. They saw the Democratic Party as the acme of democracy. Anyone was welcome to work for the party. If one worked and the party won, then he deserved a share of the spoils. To the two Irishmen this was Jacksonian Democracy in its purest form. The system was as American as apple pie; it had been around for a hundred years, and it worked. They were living proof. Both had worked hard for the party, and both were on top.

With similar backgrounds and political philosophies, it is not surprising that Pendergast shared many of Farley's joys and sorrows. He could understand why Farley worked with the urbane, well-educated Edward Flynn, but had very little empathy with him.[5] He also could understand Farley's distrust of La Guardia, and he shared the New Yorker's anger with Roosevelt for backing the mayor's candidacy. All in all, the two politicos were on the same wavelength, and it was obvious from their first meeting in New York in 1931. Farley frequently went to Kansas City. Sometimes it was on Democratic Party business, but sometimes it was just to visit. And when Pendergast suffered a heart attack in 1936, Farley left Washington as fast as possible by plane so that he could be by his friend's bedside.[6]

Among the numerous efforts Farley made in Pendergast's behalf was securing a presidential pardon for Conrad Mann. The chamber of commerce president in Kansas City, Mann had been a cohort of Pendergast for nearly twenty years. Soon after Roosevelt took office, the chamber of commerce leader was convicted of violating a lottery law and sentenced to federal prison. While Mann was on the train en route to the penitentiary, Pendergast rushed to Washington and tried to see Roosevelt about a pardon. Roosevelt refused to see the Kansas City chieftain on the grounds that he never personally took up matters of federal pardons. Not easily daunted, Pendergast sped to New York, called on his friend Farley, and even before Conrad Mann was behind the prison doors, the presidential pardon was forthcoming.[7]

Farley did still other favors for Pendergast. One of Pendergast's allies, a member of the United States House of Representatives from Missouri named Ralph Lozier, had a problem. Lozier, without any apparent success, had used his influence in Washington to get a federal position for a member of a family which had done a great deal to help him get elected. In frustration he called upon Pendergast. "I know you have great influence with Mr. Farley," wrote the congressman, "and your personal endorsement will insure Mr. Atterbury's appointment, if Mr. Farley is given to understand that you are in earnest in urging his appointment." Pendergast called upon Farley, and the postmaster general promised to do what he could. Evidently what he did was precisely what was needed, because within three months Mr. Atterbury was manager of the Home Owners' Loan Corporation at the district office in his home town.[8]

Pendergast's close relationship with James A. Farley was an important asset to the Kansas City Democratic organization. Even though Pendergast did not have the advantage of hobnobbing with the president as La Guardia did, he had the ear of one of the most powerful men in the administration. Farley's favors were extremely important to Pendergast, but equally helpful were the personal visits. Every time Farley, who was chairman of the Democratic National Committee and postmaster general of the United States, came to Kansas City, lights flashed and sirens roared. A big shot from Washington was in Kansas City —and he had come to see Big Tom.

Identification with Farley added prestige to the Pendergast machine, but probably nothing did as much to strengthen it in

Kansas City as the federal work relief programs. The skyline of
Kansas City is a lasting legacy of New Deal programs. Whoever
approaches Kansas City by automobile or airplane is struck by
a complex of skyscrapers in the heart of the business district.
Among them are the city hall, the county court house, and the
police station. The construction costs of these buildings, as well
as the city's beautiful and functional convention hall and municipal auditorium (which covers a square city block), were paid for
in part by federal grants through such agencies as PWA, CWA,
and WPA. Viewed as a whole, these structures gave Kansas City
an unusually attractive, modern face lifting. The building complex
also provided the community with facilities for conventions,
athletic events, and city and county business that were far supe-
rior to those in most cities of comparable size in the country.

Pendergast, who owned the Ready-Mixed Concrete Company,
made a small fortune from the contracts his company won to
build many of these structures. Realizing the popularity of this
immense building program, he did not hesitate to take advantage
of it. In 1938, for example, just before the city elections, the
boss ran a "Progress Edition" of the *Missouri Democrat,* a newspaper which he controlled. In this special edition were editorials
and pictures which focused on the machine-controlled city
administration and all that it had done to bring progress to the
midwestern metropolis. One section of the paper was reserved for
Ready-Mixed Concrete advertising. Beneath a photograph of the
new city hall, a structure made possible through WPA grants, appeared the following boldface line: "PERMANENCE–We are
proud to have had a part in the construction of so many Kansas
City buildings."[9]

Taking partial credit for construction programs and identifying closely with such a prominent national figure as Farley aided
the machine in innumerable ways. A form of support which was
more tangible, and for that matter ultimately more important
to the machine, was federal patronage. CWA, which lasted less
than a full year, put 100,000 men and almost 10,000 women to
work on the federal payroll in Missouri. It is impossible to say
how much of this patronage was directed by Pendergast and his
lieutenants. However, it is clear that he controlled all of Kansas
City's share of the spoils, and it was a lion's share.[10]

The single most important boost that the machine received from Washington, however, was control of the WPA. After 1935, and until it was phased out with the war, there were always 80,000 to 90,000 persons on the WPA payrolls in Missouri.[11] That Pendergast absolutely controlled this patronage and used it to strengthen his hold on the entire state is beyond question.

The director of federal work relief for Missouri was Matthew S. Murray, a Kansas Citian and close friend of Pendergast. Harry Hopkins controlled the federal work relief programs at the national level, and appointed a director for each state. Normally, the senators of each state recommended a candidate for the directorship to Hopkins, and he then gave his approval. Missouri's senators, Truman and Clark, recommended Murray only after consultation with Pendergast. Hopkins rubberstamped the recommendation.

The state director of work relief programs was a powerful person. An eminently fair director could distribute jobs and programs largely on the basis of need. But unfortunately, many state directors used the position as a political weapon. They rewarded loyal party workers with soft or high-paying jobs, channeled an inordinate amount of funds into their home counties, and even coerced rank and file employees to vote for favored candidates in primaries and general elections.[12]

Missouri's Matthew Murray was no exception. A loyal member of the Pendergast machine, he was described by one of Boss Pendergast's lieutenants as a man who has been ". . . extra close to T. J. [Pendergast], and has proved himself LOYALTY itself to the man. Murray came here thru Willie Ross of the Ross Construction Company [of which Pendergast was part owner], off the State Highway Department. . . . He was unknown to T. J. P. Yet, he played ball, made good and soon was a schooled and close-mouthed public official."[13] That Kansas City's political machine was given complete control of federal work relief programs is abundantly clear. Citizens in the state who were unemployed and seeking federal assistance often wrote to the governor, hoping he would help them find a position with the WPA. Governor Guy B. Park always replied to such inquiries by saying that the person must get in touch with Matthew S. Murray, inasmuch as he "will be in complete charge of Federal work relief in Missouri."[14] Even Senator Harry S. Truman bowed to the Pendergast machine before helping his constituents find federal jobs. To a man seeking senatorial aid in finding WPA employment, Truman replied: "If you will send us endorsements from the Kansas City Democratic Organization, I shall be glad to do what I can for you."[15]

Lloyd Stark, the man who was to be endorsed by Pendergast for governor in 1936, was told just how important the federal work relief program was to the machine. "With Murray in the saddle to see that it is administered . . . [you know] just what is to be reckoned with [because] . . . we are not fools."[16] Stark discovered what the informant meant when he ran for the gubernatorial nomination in 1936. Because he had Pendergast's endorsement, all the powers of the machine were put into action. Sworn testimony shows that WPA employees all over the state voted for Stark, and they were told they would lose their jobs if they refused.[17] In the same vein, it is clear that when he ran in the general election that same year, there were people on the federal payroll working on his behalf once again.[18]

The WPA became an integral part of Pendergast's statewide organization. In virtually every county there were federal employees who faithfully worked for the machine's candidates. The chain of command in the WPA was neatly tied into politics and usually worked quite effectively. Most district directors of WPA had their jobs because they already had put in years of loyal service with the machine. Out of appreciation for their high-paying positions, they pressured the workers in their districts to vote as they were instructed. The amount of pressure placed on the rank and file workers varied, depending upon the determination and judgment of the director involved. In many instances, employees were simply asked to vote for the organization's ticket. More aggressive directors bought their workers a beer and then asked them to vote the machine line. Some bosses were militant and threatened to fire employees who were stubborn, whereas others argued that if the machine's candidates were not elected the WPA would be removed from Missouri. Holding loss of employment over the heads of workers was exceedingly effective. Indeed, one candidate for statewide office who was opposed by Pendergast actually wrote off hopes of carrying certain counties for precisely this reason.[19]

In the final analysis, the New Deal strengthened the Pendergast machine. The favors from New Dealers such as Farley, the construction program in Kansas City and throughout the state, plus the tens of thousands of jobs on the federal payroll, all conspired to strengthen Pendergast's hold on Kansas City and Jackson County and to expand his influence all over Missouri. Machine candidates carried every election in Kansas City during the 1930s, and by higher margins each time. Likewise, Big Tom's candidates in statewide elections were almost always nominated and without exception elected until 1938.

In return for all the help which he received from the Roosevelt administration, the intense, chain-smoking boss of Kansas City delivered the votes for Roosevelt. The Missouri delegation went to the national convention in 1936 100 percent behind the president. And when election time rolled around, everyone labored diligently for the reelection of Roosevelt. Moreover, the machine delivered an overwhelming majority to the incumbent, just as it had promised.

After the election of 1936 Thomas Pendergast seemed invulnerable. His people were in every major elective and appointive office in Kansas City, Jackson County, and the state of Missouri. In addition, he was in complete control of federal work relief programs in the state. To most observers the name "Pendergast" would continue to be synonymous with power in Missouri politics because Roosevelt had been reelected, and the boss's candidate Lloyd C. Stark was ready to move into the governor's mansion.

Few Missourians would have believed in November 1936 that the fall of Pendergast was imminent—that he would be in the federal penitentiary and the machine would be a shambles in less than thirty-six months. Incredible as it may seem, it happened; and Franklin Roosevelt played no small role in the drama.

The fall of the Pendergast machine really commenced when Lloyd Stark was elected governor. Stark was a rural Missourian who had made a fortune from apples. He was the owner of Stark Brothers Nurseries, which produced the nationally famous "Stark's Delicious Apples." He was an extremely ambitious politician, but was blocked from seeking a second term in 1940 because Missouri law prohibited a governor from succeeding himself. To continue in public life in a position equal to or higher than the one he held, the apple grower had to consider the senatorial

nomination in 1940. But Harry Truman would only complete
his freshman term in 1940 and certainly would seek reelection
with the blessings of the powerful Pendergast machine.

Stark's strategy gradually became clear. What he was about
to do, and in alliance with President Roosevelt, was unbelievable
to Tom Pendergast. It is true that the Kansas City boss had voted
a few ghosts in his day. And it is true that he violated the public
trust by lining his own pockets. However, Pendergast really did
not see anything terribly wrong in that. He had, after all, spent
thousands of dollars out of his own pocket on the poor people
in Kansas City. Nobody who sought the boss's help was ever
turned away.

Furthermore, Pendergast played politics by an inflexible code
—you kept your word. If you made a promise for support, you
delivered after election day. If you accepted support, you divided
the spoils among your allies once the victory was won. The idea
of knifing a supporter in the back was totally foreign to the rules
of the political game as Pendergast played it. It was unheard of to
bite the hand that fed you. Consequently, Pendergast was un-
prepared for the attacks launched against him by Stark and Roosevelt. The Kansas City boss might have protected himself before-
hand, but he simply never believed that the man he elevated to
the state capital would try to destroy him, or that the president
he stuck his neck out for as early as 1931 would provide the
weapon.

A number of events conspired which gave Stark an opportunity
for political advancement. First of all, the federal district attorney
in Kansas City, Maurice Milligan, conducted an investigation of
the 1936 election. He discovered large-scale vote fraud and
ultimately convicted 259 of 278 defendants. These cases dragged
through the federal court for two years, all the time reminding
the public of a seamy side of the Pendergast machine.[20]

As the convictions for vote fraud piled up, many citizens
grew critical of the machine and some of its other illegal activities.
Governor Stark's office was inundated during those months with
letters from irate citizens who demanded that he clean up the
police department in Kansas City, which was protecting gambling,
prostitution, and after-hours drinking establishments.[21]

At some point Stark envisioned a plan to vault himself into

the United States Senate in 1940. If he could shroud himself
in the garb of a reformer, expose large-scale graft in the Pendergast machine, and smear Truman through guilt by association
(Pendergast hand-picked Truman for the Senate in 1934), there
would be no way to block his march to Washington. Completely
attuned to his master plan, one of Stark's close friends and
political associates who was a leader in women's Democratic
circles encouraged this ambitious coup:[22]

Now, Lloyd—please set your sails for U. S. Senator RIGHT NOW—and
keep on "sawing wood." This thing [Pendergast machine] has got to
break, and you are the ONE person to break it. . . . We are *the black spot*
in the *whole United States,* and there seems to be a silent understanding
on the part of the majority of our Democratic women, as to our goal.

Stark embarked upon a campaign where he did all he could
to attract attention to himself as a reformer and enemy of Boss
Pendergast. First he reduced Kansas City's fair share of state
patronage, and then he began firing all state employees who
had been recommended by Pendergast in the first months of the
administration. After that he launched an all-out campaign to
halt the gambling and illegal liquor traffic in Missouri's western
metropolis.[23]

Pendergast, embittered and hurt by these attacks from the
man he put into the governor's chair not long before, publicly
condemned Stark as an "ingrate."[24] But Stark, undaunted, had
just started his fight. Obviously convinced he could destroy the
big boss, his next move was for the jugular. In early 1938 the
governor and Federal District Attorney Milligan went to the
nation's capital. Feeling confident that Pendergast somewhere
along the line had misappropriated funds, they consulted the
secretary of the treasury and urged a thorough investigation of
the boss. Ultimately, Stark and Milligan were responsible for
getting T-men and the FBI to sift through every scrap of paper
in Kansas City that related to Thomas Joseph Pendergast.[25]

While this investigation was underway, the governor challenged
the boss in the primary election in August 1938. Each man put
a candidate in the primary for the state supreme court, and each
man used every tool at his disposal to win. The stakes were high.

The entire state, as well as the powers in Washington, were
watching to see if the apple grower from rural Missouri could
topple the big Irishman's urban-based machine. Pendergast put
his forces into motion. The state employees he could no longer
touch, but those holding WPA jobs were pressured to the limit.[26]
Stark, on the other hand, had the state's job holders under his
thumb. They were forced to contribute money to the campaign
fund, sport bumper stickers on their cars, and personally escort
voters to the polls.[27]

After an unusually bitter campaign Stark's candidate won
by a narrow margin. The loss was much more to Pendergast than
the supreme court slot on the Democratic ticket. Franklin D.
Roosevelt had been watching the race through his narrow political
lenses. He concluded that Pendergast was dead in Missouri, and
that Stark was the Democrat to court. Almost as soon as the
votes were tallied, the president took up with the "reform"
governor.

Farley did all that he could for Pendergast, but to no avail.
Early that year Maurice Milligan's term as federal district attorney expired, and he was to be considered for reappointment.
Senator Truman urged another appointment be made, and Farley
seconded the motion. The president, however, was "cold toward
any change in that office," according to Farley.[28]

The election scandal of 1936 had made Roosevelt less than
enthusiastic about Pendergast; hence his refusal to dump Milligan. But after Stark won the 1938 primary, Roosevelt grew
militantly anti-Pendergast. The president deliberately ignored
the wishes of the Kansas City boss on every bit of federal patronage. Realizing full well that Truman was an active member
of the machine, Roosevelt refused to approve traditionally
senatorial federal appointments which were recommended by
Truman, without first checking with Governor Stark. This infuriated Farley, who urged Roosevelt to keep in mind that a
governor should not be consulted on federal appointments. But
Roosevelt was convinced that the Missouri Democrats would
be under Stark's control by 1940, and he wanted to be in favor
with the power elite.[29]

As will be emphasized when Roosevelt's relationship with
Hague and Kelly is compared to that with Pendergast, he did not

dump the Kansas City boss because of moral indignation. Corruption he could tolerate as long as the parties involved were men of power and useful to him. By 1938 Roosevelt shunned Pendergast not because he was morally outraged, but because he believed Pendergast had become a loser.

By spring 1939 the federal investigation had paid rich dividends to Stark and Milligan. Pendergast was charged with a ten-year period of income tax evasion. The tired, sad-eyed boss pleaded guilty. Having recently suffered a severe heart attack and undergone three abdominal operations, he was not up to fighting this battle—one which he was certain to lose anyway.

Milligan, who prosecuted Pendergast, and Stark, who had instigated the drive against the boss, both were elated when the judge sentenced him to fifteen months in federal prison and five years probation thereafter. Pendergast started serving his sentence in Fort Leavenworth, Kansas, at about the same time Stark launched his campaign to unseat Harry Truman from the United States Senate.

There were two things, however, that Stark failed to count on when he deployed his grand strategy. One was that Maurice Milligan, whose name had become a household word in Missouri in the fight against Pendergast, decided to capitalize on the notoriety and try to defeat Truman himself. The second was the attitude of countless Missouri Democrats who, while they disliked the machine's corruption, still felt that Stark was a turncoat who had knifed his benefactor in the back.

Consequently, Stark lost many votes he had counted on. Some went to Milligan and still others went to Truman. Moreover, the incumbent senator won plenty of votes in his own right because he had a good record as senator and because not one breath of the machine's scandal touched him.

Truman's victory over the two "reformers" must have warmed the heart of Tom Pendergast. To be sure, there was little else to brighten those last years of his life. When he returned from prison in 1940, he brought one last wish. According to his friends, he hoped that the man he had agreed to support for the presidential nomination back in 1931 would bestow him one favor before he died. Pendergast implored Roosevelt to grant him a pardon so that he would have the rights of American citizenship once again before his death.

Wrapped in a cloak of self-righteousness, the Hyde Park aristocrat snubbed the dying Kansas City boss. Big Tom died in January 1945—his one last wish never granted. If he could have held on a few more weeks, he most certainly would have received that presidential pardon. Truman, who was elected vice president in 1944, was less than eighty days away from the presidency. That Truman would have pardoned the man who gave him his start in politics there can be little doubt. Only Vice President Truman had the courage to go to Kansas City for Pendergast's funeral. After all, said the man from Independence, "he was my friend."[30]

Just before he died, the big Irishman told a reporter from a Missouri newspaper, "I've never broken my word to any living human being I gave it to."[31] Certainly the president of the United States, who had only a few months to live himself, could never have said the same thing honestly.

6

"ROOSEVELT IS MY RELIGION"

EDWARD J. KELLY

The only representative from the Roosevelt administration who cared enough and had the courage to attend the funeral of Thomas Joseph Pendergast was Harry S. Truman. The vice president of the United States was publicly scorned for paying his last respects to the ex-con boss of Kansas City. In marked contrast, five years later was the funeral of Edward Joseph Kelly. At the Chicago boss's funeral, in the words of one of the thousands of mourners, ". . . a cardinal gave his eulogy, President Truman sent an emissary [Attorney General S. Howard McGrath], and a governor [Adlai E. Stevenson] and a United States Senator [Paul H. Douglas] led a three-block line of men who had owed him personal allegiance."[1]

Fate had been good to Edward Kelly, much better than it had been to Tom Pendergast. By the time the Democratic National Convention adjourned in 1932, Pendergast was in command of a powerful machine which had backed Roosevelt down the line. Kelly, on the other hand, was merely a high-level associate of Mayor Anton Cermak, who had been in power only one year, whose organization was just beginning to jell, and who had made the political blunder of refusing to endorse Roosevelt on the early ballots at Chicago.

To say the very least, it is unusual that a man in Kelly's second-string position should end up as one of the most powerful and respected Democrats in the United States only three years

after Governor Roosevelt's presidential nomination. Kelly, however, was an Irish Catholic who must have carried a shamrock
blessed by the Pope himself in his coat pocket.

The Kelly success story began right after the national convention. Jim Farley and Roosevelt were cool toward Mayor Cermak
and all his lieutenants. Still, they had no intention of permanent-
ly snubbing the Chicago organization. After all, Illinois had gone
Democrat in a presidential election only twice since the Civil
War. If Chicago and Cook County failed the Democratic nominee,
he had little chance of carrying Illinois.

Apparently sometime between the convention and late August,
Cermak and the man destined to be his successor, Ed Kelly, visited Roosevelt at Hyde Park. What they discussed is not known,
but no doubt it revolved around Cermak's reputation with Roosevelt.[2] The conference obviously improved Cermak's standing
with Roosevelt because Farley announced that Chicago's mayor,
rather than a preconvention Roosevelt supporter, would direct
the national campaign in Illinois. Although in directing the
campaign he delivered twice the 200,000 majority he had promised,
Boss Cermak was uneasy. And rightly so, because there was talk
that Senator J. Hamilton Lewis was to be awarded the honor of
distributing the federal patronage for all of Illinois. Cermak was
worried about the federal patronage, and he made his fears known
to his associates. Consequently, he went to Florida in February
1933 to confer with Farley and the president-elect. Cermak
saw Farley first, and Farley reassured him. Then the mayor went
to see Roosevelt to get Farley's promises confirmed. It was the
night of 15 February 1933. Cermak and several other dignitaries
sat in the grandstand at Miami's Bayfront Park listening to Roosevelt speak. Once Roosevelt finished, Cermak and the others walked
out to shake his hand and chat. While Cermak talked to Roosevelt, a mentally-ill Calabrian immigrant, Guiseppe Zangara, fired
several shots at Roosevelt. He missed his target completely, but
hit Cermak and four others. Three weeks later Cermak died.[3]

Cermak's death marked the beginning of a new era between
the Chicago Democratic machine and Franklin D. Roosevelt.
The man who assumed the assassinated mayor's position was
destined to become a friend and advisor to the president, the
machine would be unyielding in its support for Roosevelt, and

all concerned were to be amply rewarded. That new man was Edward J. Kelly, a fifty-seven-year-old chief engineer of the Chicago Sanitary District. Born in the "back-of-the-yards" (stockyards) section of Chicago, Kelly never had an opportunity to finish grammar school. Like many city bosses of his era, he worked full-time from boyhood and entered politics as an escape from the drudgery of manual labor. A bright, articulate young man with unbounded energy and ambition, he first became involved in politics while he was attending night school and studying engineering. Upon assuming the position of the city's chief engineer in 1920, he met another active Democrat, Patrick Nash. Nash was a sewer contractor. Between 1920 and 1933 they became close friends and political associates, and Nash did over $100 million of construction for the district. When Cermak died, Nash, who was by that time the chairman of the Cook County Democratic Committee and certainly one of the most powerful Democrats in the state, convinced the City Council to name Kelly interim mayor until the city election of 1935.[4]

Kelly was elected in his own right in 1935, and this position, with over 30,000 patronage jobs plus the incredible support he ultimately received from the Roosevelt administration, entrenched him as one of the most powerful city bosses in the history of the United States. His relationship with Roosevelt had started before Cermak's death. The rather distinguished looking, bespectacled chief engineer had gone with Cermak to Hyde Park the summer after the national convention. Between the Hyde Park meeting and the November election, Kelly wrote a long letter to Roosevelt. In this letter he candidly evaluated the Democratic nominee's campaign speechmaking tactics and suggested that less emphasis be placed on criticizing the Republican Party. Instead, he suggested, criticize Hoover personally, because there were many Republicans who disliked Hoover and might well vote for Roosevelt if he refrained from attacking their party. Roosevelt viewed Kelly's comments as "very helpful." And as time passed, he would eagerly seek more of the Chicago leader's opinions and advice.[5]

What Roosevelt liked about Kelly was that he was brutally frank—even if it was unflattering. This first letter established that fact. Sam Rosenman, one of Roosevelt's speech writers and advisors, remembered, as we have seen, that his boss "always tried to get the truth. There were some . . . on whom he could always rely for frank and accurate appraisals, no matter how brutal they might be." One of those few candid observers, according to Rosenman, was Kelly.[6]

It would be misleading to assume that immediately after Kelly's letter reached Roosevelt during the campaign in 1932, the president-to-be took him on as an advisor and insider. On the contrary, while Roosevelt was impressed with the Cermak aide, he was not about to form a close alliance with any of the Chicago Democrats. After all, Cermak had defeated the Republican machine of "Big Bill" Thompson only as recently as 1931. Despite the fact that Cermak was mayor and had put together an apparently effective organization of his own, no one in the Roosevelt circle was certain who would hold the reins of the Illinois Democrats.

Furthermore, when Cermak died and Kelly was appointed mayor, a feud developed between the Democratic governor, Henry Horner, and the Cook County organization, which was then under the aegis of Kelly and Nash. The governor and the mayor both wanted control of Illinois's federal patronage, but Hopkins, as well as Roosevelt and Farley, went into a period of watchful waiting to see who would emerge the power in the party. Hoping to avoid alienating either faction, they divided the control of FERA and CWA patronage between the two, with Kelly getting the edge in Cook County and Horner downstate.[7]

In early 1935 two impressive showings by Mayor Kelly caught the politically directed eyes of Hopkins and Roosevelt sufficiently for them to decide to throw their lot in with him. Kelly had to run for election in his own right in 1935, and his first hurdle was the primary. The University of Chicago professor Paul H. Douglas, an idealist and self-styled reformer, had no doubt observed the New York City mayoralty race with great interest. Roosevelt had been behind La Guardia and the Fusion ticket in a war against Tammany Hall. Inasmuch as Professor A. A. Berle had been the liaison man between La Guardia and the president, Professor Douglas may have assumed that Roosevelt would like to block the ambitions of another Democratic machine. But it should be recalled from chapter 4 that Roosevelt was not out to smash the city machines per se. He attacked or defended them primarily on his judgment as to who could further his own ambitions.

In any case, Douglas tried to put together a fusion ticket in Chicago, with another professor, Charles Merriam, to head it against the Kelly-Nash organization. Douglas thought he could get White House endorsement of his pie-in-the-sky movement. He found, of course, only deaf ears in Washington. Kelly went on to impress Roosevelt with an overwhelming primary victory, which he followed up with the most lopsided general election victory in Chicago's history. He defeated his opponent by winning over 75 percent of the vote.[8]

This demonstration of the machine's power was followed by Kelly's intervention in the state legislature on the side of Harry Hopkins. The Federal Relief Administration had been plagued with the inability or unwillingness of Governor Horner to raise the necessary funds to accompany federal expenditures in the state. Horner's recalcitrance after numerous promises forced Hopkins to cut off federal funds to the state. This drastic action brought loud cries of anguish, and Hopkins was called every name in the book by irate citizens and journalists. The problem was ultimately resolved when Mayor Kelly threw his weight behind Hopkins and pressured and cajoled the legislature into raising the money.[9]

After taking the pressure off Hopkins through this action with the legislators, and after his overwhelming mayoralty victory, Kelly proved he was the boss of an organization which could deliver when it counted. Jim Farley applauded Kelly for a "splendid victory," and Hopkins called the Chicago mayor to Washington for a conference. The result was well put by Gene Jones, an historian who carefully examined the intricacies of these 1935 events: they "cemented" relations between Kelly and the Roosevelt administration.[10]

The "cement" which bound Roosevelt and Kelly set quickly as the president eyed the national convention and election only a year away. Almost overnight, Kelly had proved himself the power in Cook County—and without Cook County, Roosevelt could not have the Illinois delegation behind his nomination and those electoral votes in his column the following November.

Among the numerous favors bestowed upon Boss Kelly by
Roosevelt and his associates was control of the WPA. Robert
Dunham, a loyal Kelly man, was made Illinois's first director
of Federal Work Relief in mid-1935. Control of WPA, of course,
was extremely important to the Cook County organization. The
total number of men and women employed by WPA fluctuated
(there were 199,823 in 1936, 181,938 in 1938, and 180,965 in
1940), but it always crowded 200,000, and only New York and
Pennsylvania had more people on the federal payroll.[11] That
Kelly's machine controlled this patronage there is no doubt. The
mayor's rival for party domination, Henry Horner, was terribly
angry about the WPA. He told Harold Ickes that Hopkins ignored
him. Indeed, he could never even get him on the phone; whereas
Hopkins always consulted Kelly.[12]

Governor Horner's anger toward the WPA in Illinois continued
to grow. He encouraged Senator J. Hamilton Lewis to support
a bill in Congress which would have placed all state directors of
WPA under the thumb of the governors.[13] Likewise he did his
best to embarrass Hopkins by crippling the relief programs out
of spite.[14] Furthermore, he informed Farley that WPA was hurting the national administration with the voters in Illinois because
of "certain incompetents in charge."[15]

These tirades had little effect on anyone in Washington. Even
though there was concrete evidence that the machine's lieutenants
pressured WPA workers to contribute money to campaigns and
to vote for the organization's candidates under the threat of losing their jobs, nothing at all was done to discipline the violators
or punish the Cook County machine.[16] On the contrary, Harry
Hopkins not only stood by Kelly and company, he did what he
could to provide them with *extra* money. In December 1936
Hopkins phoned state director Dunham and told him: ". . . The
Treasury has suddenly found a little more money, and I don't
want to put you and Ed in a hot spot. If there is any money here
and it will do some good, I want you to have it." He promised
to deliver a sum of $750,000 if it "would be reflected mainly
in Chicago."[17]

Hopkins was not the only person in the administration who
recognized Kelly's power and conducted business primarily
through him. The state's attorney for Illinois complained that

"Farley never talks with anyone in Chicago except Mayor Kelly."[18] The correspondence between Farley and Kelly during those years shows that despite all of his disclaimers about favoritism in Illinois, Jim Farley was 100 percent behind the mayor of Chicago and his close associate Pat Nash.[19] Farley even became party to Kelly's attempt to destroy Governor Horner by not supporting him for renomination in 1936. In December 1935 Roosevelt visited Chicago. The Cook County machine held a luncheon in the president's honor but refused to invite Governor Horner. After that luncheon, where Kelly and Nash sat on either side of the president, Roosevelt offered Horner a federal judgeship, and Kelly and Nash told the governor they could not endorse him in the 1936 primary.[20]

Horner refused to be intimidated. He ran against Kelly's forces in the Democratic primary and won, despite the fact that he did not have White House blessing. The evidence shows that WPA workers all over Illinois were told to vote for Kelly's gubernatorial candidate (Herman Bundesen), and many were assessed for the campaign fund.[21] Governor Horner used similar tactics in the battle himself. Despite his campaign image of a reformer out to smash the coercive city machine, he used his control over patronage in a way which made it clear there was no qualitative difference between the so-called reformer Horner and Boss Kelly. The governor had 95 of 102 county chairmen on his payroll, and he did not hesitate to push them into line. He also relieved a number of state employees of their jobs because they were known supporters of the Kelly machine. Furthermore, the "reformer" did not hesitate to use the taxpayers' money to support the "Horner for Governor Club." Thousands of two-page letters were mailed to citizens all over Illinois from this partisan club, and the bonded paper they used bore the seal of Illinois in the watermark.[22]

The historian James T. Patterson summed up the primary contest very well. "The dispute," he wrote "which some described as a battle between a corrupt urban machine and a more progressively inclined governor, was really a power contest between two opponents, each of whom pined for recognition from Washington."[23] Seen in this light, the Kelly-Horner feud in the 1936 primary was identical to the Stark-Pendergast battle in Missouri in 1938. A significant difference in outcome between the contests, however,

is that Pendergast's defeat led to the end of his alliance with
Roosevelt, whereas Horner's victory over Kelly had no such
consequence for Chicago's mayor.

There are several reasons why Franklin Roosevelt did not
desert Kelly and throw his support to Horner after the Illinois
primary. To have changed loyalties in Illinois would not have
been politically advantageous as it was in Missouri. Pendergast
was losing his following because of election frauds which were
in the headlines every day. Governor Stark was actually winning
many Democrats to his anti-Pendergast cause. As a matter of
fact, it was apparent to Roosevelt that Stark had more Democrats rallying to his faction in 1938 than Pendergast. Kelly, on
the other hand, was still the Democrat in Illinois with the most
votes. It is true that Horner won the renomination, but the
Cook County machine won every race in the primary except the
gubernatorial. Although Horner nosed out the machine in the
downstate districts because of Republican and anti-New Deal
sympathy, the machine delivered for Bundesen in Cook County.
And Roosevelt still had to carry Cook County if he hoped to
carry Illinois in 1936. Kelly could help Roosevelt there, but
Horner could not do him much good. Therefore, inasmuch as
Horner's strength was in downstate Illinois, and especially
among anti–New Dealers to begin with, Roosevelt saw absolutely
no advantage in breaking his alliance with Kelly.[24]

For purely practical political reasons, then, Roosevelt and
his coterie of advisors remained aligned with the Cook County
machine. Some of those in the president's inner circle had their
own personal reasons as well for staying on the good side of
Edward Kelly. It is no secret that Jim Farley had his eye on the
Democratic nomination in 1940. Completely loyal to Roosevelt
in 1936, Farley assumed the president would step down in 1940.
With this goal in sight, it is not surprising that Farley would do
all in his power to keep on the good side of the mayor of Chicago.[25]

Hopkins was another insider with his eye on the White House
in 1940. Like Farley, Hopkins was intent on cultivating all the
big city bosses in hopes of having their states' delegates in his
hip pocket in the scramble for the nomination once Roosevelt
stepped down. The image of Hopkins as the idealistic social
worker is not at all accurate. The minister of relief was shrewd

and cynical, and he had his eye on the 1940 presidential nomination until his duodenal ulcer got so bad that he had to have a sizable part of his stomach removed. By early 1938 he was still making overtures toward the nomination although he probably knew it was all over for him because of poor health.[26]

By the mid-1930s, then, Edward J. Kelly was undisputed boss of Chicago and Cook County. Patrick Nash, the chairman of the county committee and national committeeman, was not without some say, but he was in his early seventies and not as active as he had been in the old days. Kelly, on the other hand, had just turned sixty. He was in good shape, and looked and acted younger than he was. The vibrant mayor had come a long way from his poverty-stricken boyhood in the "back-of-the-yard" district.

Patrick Nash had hand-picked him to succeed Cermak as mayor in 1933, which was tantamount to making him the boss of Cook County. By astutely providing services for most of the numerous hyphenated-American groups in Chicago—the Lithuanians, Yugoslavs, Poles, Germans, Swedes, Irish, Jews, Czechs—just as Cermak had done, Kelly held together the organization he inherited. But he went farther. He also worked hard to win over the Italians and blacks, most of whom had supported the Republicans while Cermak was in power. Through night school, hard work, and determination, Kelly became a competent civil engineer and an urbane and sophisticated gentleman. These dimensions to his character provided entry into the business community where he ultimately found many friends and supporters.[27]

Kelly built a machine by providing services for the citizens of Chicago and Cook County. Certainly, he alienated some people, but to the majority he gave what they wanted. And with Franklin D. Roosevelt, Harry L. Hopkins, and James A. Farley all seeking his friendship, Kelly received even more than the city and county purse strings and patronage could provide him for organization building.

The New Dealers gave Kelly more than all of the previously noted WPA patronage, which ran between 180,000 and 200,000 jobs per year. Besides that, Chicago received millions of dollars in direct relief. These funds, which poured in before WPA was

launched in 1935, were a real boon to Kelly. Gene Jones, a
student of the Chicago mayor's administration, said that FERA
funds saved the city millions of dollars. "Federal aid had provided the wherewithal for them [Kelly machine] to weather the
first years of economic crisis. This help," Jones continued, "enabled Kelly during his first two years at City Hall to establish a
reputation for efficiency and, in a sense, bought time necessary
for the machine to consolidate its political success."[28]

Beyond these early years the New Deal brought still more
benefits. Harold L. Ickes remembered that Roosevelt was quite
anxious to see federal money spent on the public projects Kelly
wanted for Chicago, even though Ickes warned him that 20
percent of the expenditures would go for graft.[29] Countless
public improvement programs were undertaken in Chicago. Kelly
did his best to explain the benefits of these programs to his
constituents and to identify himself and his administration with
those projects while still giving Washington some credit too.[30]

President Roosevelt was keenly aware of the political benefits
one could derive from these federally sponsored public improvement projects. Sometimes he made "inspection" tours of construction sites, or occasionally he dedicated a construction site
himself. In this way he focused attention on himself and the
New Deal, as well as on any local officials he might want to
favor by having them with him on the tour or the platform. If
Roosevelt could not be in a community to take personal advantage of a ribbon cutting, he might help a political ally by sending
a telegram which could be read to the crowd at the dedication.
In 1938, for example, Roosevelt saw no way to get to Chicago
for the grand opening of the $18-million PWA-supported subway.
He did, however, send Kelly a telegram which said, "The new
subway represents a fine achievement for the City of Chicago
and your administration."[31] This was precisely what the mayor
wanted all Chicagoans to believe. The particular wording of the
telegram was no accident. The president's secretary told him
before sending it that "a pat on the back [for Kelly] will be very
helpful" inasmuch as some political opponents of the mayor's
were trying to give all the credit for the subway to Harold Ickes
the secretary of the interior.[32]

Little gestures such as this telegram from the president, when added to Kelly's natural affinity for New Deal measures, nurtured in the mayor a deep and abiding affection for Roosevelt. One of Kelly's cohorts said, "Kelly was just nuts about Roosevelt, sincerely so. He had a speech he always delivered—'Roosevelt Is My Religion.' "[33] Roosevelt liked Kelly, too. No city boss except Ed Flynn, and possibly La Guardia, ever got so close to Roosevelt. The president saw Curley once or twice after 1933, but their relationship was like ice. He avoided contacts with Hague and Pendergast and only chatted briefly with Crump on one or two occasions.

The president valued Kelly's sagacity and his ability to get his fingers on the pulse beat of Illinois and the entire nation. Consequently, he often used him as a sounding board or put issues out to the mayor as trial balloons before taking a stand in public.[34] But Roosevelt saw Kelly as more than an advisor—he genuinely enjoyed his companionship. The Chicago mayor occasionally lunched with Roosevelt both in Washington and in Hyde Park, and the two exchanged warm notes at Christmas time. There is every reason to believe that Roosevelt's note to Kelly in 1943 came right from the heart: "Your re-election makes your old friend very happy."[35]

Even Eleanor Roosevelt liked Kelly. While she usually avoided the hard-core Irish politicos—a group she felt was a rather boorish lot—she saw Kelly, along with Ed Flynn, as an exception. By no means a woman who would go out of her way for one of Franklin's associates she didn't like, Mrs. Roosevelt actually endorsed Kelly publicly in 1940 when many journalists were trying to demean him as a corrupt boss of the Hague-Pendergast variety. The president's wife was soundly attacked for this warm gesture. But it made no difference; Kelly had a progressive record as mayor, and the First Lady unflinchingly pointed it out.[36]

If Ed Kelly had not been a bright, personable chap, there were plenty of other reasons for Roosevelt to align forces with him. He promised to deliver Cook County to Roosevelt each time that he ran for reelection, and he did so faithfully. If he had not put Illinois into the Democratic column in 1936, 1940, and once again in 1944, Roosevelt would not have been attracted by any degree of charm. But Kelly always produced a large enough vote in Cook County to put the Democratic Party over in Illinois.

Kelly did still other other things to repay Roosevelt for all the help he gave the Cook County machine. Besides turning out the vote at election time, Kelly had Illinois delegates in line for Roosevelt each time he sought renomination. While this in itself was invaluable, Kelly's role in the 1940 national convention was colossal. Well before July 1940 the mayor organized a nation-wide "Draft Roosevelt" movement. Roosevelt was well aware of this action and did absolutely nothing to stop it. On the contrary, while the president never came right out and said, "I want a third term," he made it known that he could be drafted but was not actively seeking the nomination.

Roosevelt was always sly. Indeed, he was a genius when it came to politics. That he wanted to be reelected for a third term is almost certain. It is true that he did not play an active and open role in securing the nomination as he had done in 1932 and 1936, but then 1940 was for an unprecedented third term. He certainly did not want to appear presumptuous. If drafted, on the other hand, he would be forced to accept the nomination out of duty to party and country.

Chicago's mayor was hardly obtuse when it came to politics. He knew Roosevelt wanted a third term, but he recognized it had to look like a draft by popular demand. Kelly therefore or-ganized the "Draft Roosevelt" movement without a word of protest from the White House. Instead, the president made him a gift of a Panama hat, ostensibly a token of thanks for some political business the mayor handled for him in Florida, but more likely a subtle way to say, "Thanks and keep up the good work."[37]

The task of getting the convention to draft Roosevelt was no small one. Ed Flynn, who was not overly enthusiastic about a third term himself, recalled that "a majority of the delegates were not enthusiastically for the renomination of the President. . . ."[38] Regardless of the possible pitfalls that lay ahead, Boss Kelly moved on with his plans. In mid-June he was summoned by Roose-velt to the White House. The green light was switched on.[39]

Complicating Kelly's task was Jim Farley. As chairman of the National Committee, Farley had friends in every state of the union, and many were in positions to control delegates. It seems that the president had not been candid with Farley on the ques-tion of running for reelection. The ambitious Irishman asked

Roosevelt if he intended to seek a third term, and if not, could he count on his endorsement? Roosevelt never promised to back Farley, but he did assure him that he would not seek reelection.[40] After receiving this assurance in early 1940, Farley remained steadfast. He was going to the convention at Chicago opposed to a third term for Roosevelt and with his own hat in the ring.

In retrospect it is easy to understand why Roosevelt selected Chicago for the Democratic convention in 1940. What better place than Kelly's home ground, when he was to be in charge of the "spontaneous draft"? A writer for the *New Republic* pointed out that at the "convention in Mr. Kelly's Chicago, the New Deal forces will have to have a floor commander, tough-minded, shrewd, indefatigable, who will be able to talk to the exceedingly practical-minded gentlemen who will form a large portion of the delegates. Inasmuch as Farley is opposed to the President's nomination, Mr. Kelly seemed the natural choice."[41]

Kelly turned out to be the perfect choice for the third-term forces. Before the convention assembled, he lined up a number of the city bosses in his camp. Among them were Frank Hague, Edward Crump, and Tom Pendergast's nephew James Pendergast. He knew he could count on Ed Flynn, and he knew Fiorello La Guardia was doing everything in power to sway New York. Flynn assessed the conveners in this way:[42]

The persons in the forefront in support of the President's ambition for a third term were largely drawn from the political machines of the country. Again I say they did not support Roosevelt out of any motive or affection or because of any political issues involved, but rather they knew that opposing him would be harmful to their local organizations. The Roosevelt name would help more than it could hurt, and for that reason these city leaders went along on the third-term candidacy.

With this hard core of delegates behind him, Kelly made the next step toward Roosevelt's nomination. He realized that most delegates were not in favor of a third term. However, there was no single contender for the nomination (including Farley) who could immediately unite the party. Kelly thought that if he could start a demonstration for Roosevelt just before the balloting began, he could pull plenty of potential opponents into the "draft." They would probably rather go along with Roosevelt again than see the party hopelessly torn assunder.

With clocklike precision Ed Kelly put his machine together. First of all, he gave Harry Hopkins (who had been in on the plan from the outset) a courtesy badge as a deputy sergeant-at-arms, so that he could get on the floor and organize forces for Roosevelt. Hopkins was not a delegate and otherwise would not have been able to get in. Kelly also packed the galleries with the rank and file of his own Cook County machine. The next step was Kelly's own welcoming speech, which he delivered on the first night. Although his remarks were short, his address sounded more like a nomination speech for Roosevelt than it did a word of welcome to the delegates.

On the second night, just before the balloting and at the outset of the speech putting Farley's name in nomination, the gallery broke out into cheers of "We want Roosevelt." Then when a message from Roosevelt stating that he was not seeking a third term was read, a voice boomed over a loud speaker through the ventilation system, "We want Roosevelt." Opponents of Roosevelt and the third term dubbed it the "voice from the sewer." The voice, of course, belonged to one of Kelly's henchmen who delivered the cheer as a signal to Kelly supporters in each delegation and the gallery to start a massive "spontaneous" demonstration. The scheduled "show" lasted just seven minutes short of a full hour. Chaos followed for some time, just as planned. When the balloting began, Roosevelt won the nomination by getting over 900 ballots to 72 for Farley, his closest rival.[43]

The 1940 Democratic National Convention was as rigged or controlled as the infamous one of 1968. The Chicago Mayor Richard J. Daley did the rigging in 1968, but he took lessons from Mayor Kelly. Daley was there in 1940, as one of Kelly's lieutenants. Indeed, the man who was the leader of the Cook County machine was an efficient and loyal member of it in Kelly's halcyon days. It was boss-to-be Daley, it should be realized, who took his cues from Kelly in 1943 in the Illinois state legislature. Daley was a state senator, and he led the fight which blocked the roll call of all senators on the question of an anti-fourth-term resolution. Daley saved the day for Democrats who were unwilling to go on record about a fourth term over a year before it was convention time again.[44]

Roosevelt appreciated Kelly's supreme efforts in his behalf in 1940. To the Chicago boss it had been an honor and a privilege. He once wrote to Roosevelt: "I can only say that I deem it a distinct privilege to be at your call and service in any manner at any time. I welcome such an opportunity beyond measure of expression."[45] Kelly meant it. Whereas Flynn surmised that most of the bosses who threw their support behind Roosevelt in 1940 died it only for what was in it for them, Kelly did it for love as much as for political gain.

Edward Joseph Kelly had been 100 percent behind Roosevelt ever since stepping into the mayor's office in 1933. He produced the delegates for Roosevelt in 1936, 1940, and again in 1944; and he put Illinois into Roosevelt's camp at November each time, too. In addition, Kelly frequently went to the White House and Hyde Park to advise the Chief on political strategy and to discuss the issues of the day. It should be remembered that Kelly delivered hundreds of speeches for Roosevelt, and he relentlessly poured his energy into every campaign. Furthermore, any time Roosevelt worried about a bill going through the Congress, Kelly put pressure to bear on the senators and congressmen from Illinois who were in his debt for their elections.[46]

Because Boss Kelly of Chicago could be depended upon—because no other Democrat successfully challenged him for control of Cook County's Democrats—Roosevelt befriended him and continued to bestow favors. The result was that when the mayor retired from public life in 1947, he retired a winner. Moreover, he left the legacy of a machine that had grown sleeker and fatter from New Deal plums, and that existed under the direction of Richard J. Daley until he died in December 1976. However the course of Chicago politics is difficult to predict at this time since Mayor Daley died leaving as his legacy a power struggle for party control.

7

FRANK HAGUE

William Dean Howells once said that "the kindlier view of any man is apt to be the truer view." Maybe this is true, but it is difficult to apply to Frank Hague. Aside from a 1937 feature article in the already disreputable *Literary Digest* (the *Digest's* days were numbered after it predicted that Landon would defeat Roosevelt in 1936), most journalists portrayed the boss of Jersey City as a "Dictator—American Style" or "King Hanky-Panky." Hague's city, it was argued, was an "occupied area" under the rule of New Jersey's "Hitler."[1]

There is some truth in this popular picture of Hague, but like most such images, it is not completely accurate. Hague was no angel, but he always had a large popular following. One of the reasons people in Jersey City liked Frank Hague was because they could identify with his humble beginnings in the Horseshoe section of south Jersey City. The Horseshoe got its name in 1871 after the Republicans gerrymandered most of the city's Democrats into one assembly district, bordered by Hoboken on the north and the Hudson River on the east, and rounded off to the west and south in a horseshoe shape.

In 1876, the year Hague was born, Jersey City's population was approximately 120,000. About one-fifth of this number was foreign born, and many of those came from Ireland. Most of the immigrants and native-born laborers were forced to raise their families in the Horseshoe, close to their places of employment, where rent was the lowest. It was down among the railroad yards, noisy wharves, and soot-blackened factories that Frank Hague was born. Although most of the neighbors lived in crowded tenements, Frank's Irish-born father managed to move his Irish bride and eight children into a dilapidated frame house when he became a guard at a local bank.[2]

Frank nearly died as an infant, a fate which would not have been unusual in a late nineteenth-century city, especially among slum children. But he had a strong constitution and grew into a tall, lean, strong boy with sandy-colored hair and piercing blue eyes. A typical rowdy of the Horseshoe, Hague ran in a gang, swam in the river, and fought in the streets. His mother saw to it that he regularly attended mass, but no one succeeded in getting him to school very often. Indeed, in the sixth grade at the age of fourteen he was expelled for habitual truancy, and thus ended his formal schooling. From Public School 21 he went to work as a blacksmith's helper, and then took an unskilled job with the Erie Railroad. In his spare time he worked out in a gymnasium and became a rather good boxer. While fighting in the gym, he met a professional lightweight fighter named Joe Craig. Looking for an opportunity to get out of the railroad yards and into a suit and tie, Hague made a deal with Craig, became his manager, and was able to turn his back on work clothes and common labor forever.[3]

During those years as Craig's manager Hague became well known in the Horseshoe. He spent many hours around the Cable Athletic Club and the Greenwood Social Club, where he distinguished himself as the local fashion plate in impeccably clean shirts and four-buttoned, double-breasted plaid suits. Those who knew him believed his ambitions to be modest. He wanted to avoid manual labor, to dress smartly, and eventually to get a job on the police force. As a matter of fact, he demonstrated no particular interest in politics, and entered it unexpectedly on the initiative of others. Hague's political career began when a well-known saloonkeeper in the Horseshoe, Nat Kenny, decided to challenge the Democratic boss of the neighborhood, Denny McLaughlin. Kenny had no interest in holding public office himself, but he wanted to become the behind-the-scenes power of the Horseshoe Democrats. McLaughlin held no public office either, but he had many friends in the area and could deliver a large bloc of votes for candidates of his own choice at election time.

Just prior to a special election in 1896 to elect constables and members of the street and water board, Kenny was searching for some men who were popular in the Horseshoe. It was suggested that young Frank Hague, who was well known in the clubs and the fight world, would be a good choice to run for constable. Hague was asked to run; he accepted and went on to win.[4]

This victory was all Hague needed to realize that his calling was politics. The man of modest ambitions quickly developed a monumental appetite for power and prestige. He worked faithfully for the regular Democratic organization until Jersey City got caught up in the nationwide clamor for reform. Consequently, in 1913 Hague became a reformer. He called for cleaning the "bosses" out of city hall and bringing honesty and efficiency to city government. The boy from the Horseshoe won the election and became a city commissioner; then he became mayor of Jersey City. Once in the mayor's office, he stayed until his voluntary retirement in 1947.[5]

During these early years in the mayor's office, Hague carefully attended to the business of building a political machine. He enlarged his following by modernizing the city's fire and police departments. Eventually he had lieutenants in every ward of the city. Their job was to care for the needy and then get out the vote on election day. In middle class neighborhoods the boss established social clubs where people could relax and play. For the business community, both small and large, there were tax breaks and other favors. Hague also had the patent support of the Roman Catholic Church in Jersey City. The boss contributed large sums of money and some magnificent gifts to the church, and in return he had its endorsement at election time. Deliberate efforts were made to do favors for Jews and Protestants. Several well-known and influential rabbis and Protestant ministers were on the city payroll as "utility men" or "special inspectors."[6]

By the time Roosevelt launched the New Deal, Hague was a powerful and popular mayor with an efficient and loyal organization at his command. The seamier side of his character and the most ruthless tactics of his machine had not yet come to light. As explained in chapter 1, Hague had emerged the leader of the New Jersey Democratic Party by 1932, and he went to the national convention at Chicago militantly anti-Roosevelt. His idol was Al Smith, and Frank Hague used every ounce of influence at his disposal to see him nominated.

If Roosevelt had been inclined to hold a grudge against anyone in Al Smith's camp, it would have been toward Hague. The arrogant, wisecracking boss of Jersey City was Smith's floor manager at the convention, and it was he who told reporters in Chicago that Roosevelt, if nominated, would not carry even one state east of the Mississippi.

This was a big crow to swallow, but Hague was an audacious man with enough appetite for the task. Immediately after the convention Jim Farley went to Atlantic City to rest and recuperate from the strain and pressure of the battle for the nomination. He was not there long before he received a phone call from Hague. "He said," Farley remembered, "there was no soreness on his part over what had happened, that he was whipped in a fair fight, and that if Governor Roosevelt would come to New Jersey to open his campaign, he would provide the largest political rally ever held in the United States."[7]

Regardless of how much bitterness Roosevelt felt toward Hague, one thing was certain, he was not about to seek revenge. New Jersey, after all, was a populous state with a sizable bloc of electoral votes. With the exception of one senatorial and two gubernatorial races, New Jersey had voted Republican for every major candidate, including president, since the end of World War I. To refuse the aid of the state's most powerful Democrat would be suicidal. There was no hope of carrying New Jersey without Frank Hague's endorsement.

Always the realist, Roosevelt grasped the olive branch, accepted Hague's invitation, and opened his presidential campaign with a speech delivered in front of Governor A. Harry Moore's home at Sea Girt. Jim Farley estimated that between 100,000 and 115,000 people were present to hear Roosevelt at what *was* probably the largest political rally ever to take place in the United States.[8] Roosevelt was markedly impressed by the demonstration. If Hague could do this, he probably could put the state in the Democratic column in November. The boss of Jersey City was speaking the nominee's language, and it appeared that the hatchet was buried forever. Indeed, some months after the general election, when Hague had delivered the vote for Roosevelt, he wrote a note to the president. "Your recognition of our State Organization has been substantially manifested and in return I feel we owe you this pledge of loyalty. Should the occasion ever arise when New Jersey need be counted, I am yours to command."[9]

This letter reveals the heart of the Roosevelt-Hague relationship. Hague delivered the vote as promised in 1932. In return the president showered the New Jersey boss with favors. As long as the favors poured in, Hague would use his machine to support Roosevelt, and as long as Roosevelt needed Hague, the favors would be forthcoming.

Concrete evidence shows that from the outset of the New Deal, Frank Hague was in complete control of all federal patronage in the state. Federal appointments were not filtered through the governor or New Jersey's senators. On the contrary, the mayor of Jersey City made all the decisions. Governor A. Harry Moore was inundated with appeals for help in finding various kinds of federal jobs. Almost invariably he answered the applicants in the way he wrote to a Newark man in August 1933. "I do not have the power," explained the governor, "to appoint to these Federal positions. They are made upon the recommendation of the local organizations to Mayor Hague, who, in turn, sends them in. . . . I would suggest that you also get in touch with the mayor."[10]

When Hague wrote to Roosevelt that "your recognition of our State Organization has been substantially manifested," he implied that everyone in the Roosevelt administration was being generous. It seems no one wanted to offend Frank Hague and his organization. Jim Farley did his best to help if the cause was legitimate. The postmaster general believed in party regularity. The Hague machine had put Roosevelt over in New Jersey, so it deserved New Jersey's share of the spoils. Typical of Farley's willingness to go to bat for the machine was an incident in 1934. Hague's puppet, Governor A. Harry Moore, called upon Farley to use his influence to restore a friend to a CWA post as an aeronautical inspector. It seems that the man was competent, but

that his services were already covered by others in the state.
Farley took the case to the secretary of commerce, who controlled
appointments of this rank. Although the man did not get his old
job back, he was given another post of equal caliber.[11]

It is true that Farley always worked well with the big city
bosses. He talked their language, believed in party organization,
and held with the philosophy that the winners should take the
spoils. As mentioned in connection with the 1940 national convention in chapter 6, it is also true that Farley hoped to become
president and believed his long-time friendship with the bosses
would enhance his chances. However, there were limits to which
Farley would go to win political support. There is no question
about it, Jim Farley was a man of unimpeachable integrity. An
issue surrounding Farley and Hague which sheds light on this point
came in the late 1930s, after Hague had faithfully delivered the
delegates and the votes in two presidential contests. As postmaster
general, Farley learned that Frank Hague had one of his henchmen opening every piece of mail that went to or came from one
of his political enemies. In a fit of anger the usually jovial Farley
stormed in to see the president for orders on how to proceed with
arrest and prosecution. To Farley's disappointment, Roosevelt
said: "Forget prosecution. You go tell Frank to knock it off.
We can't have this kind of thing going on. But keep this quiet.
We need Hague's support if we want New Jersey."[12]

Harry Hopkins did his best to curry favor with Frank Hague.
An ex–social worker, Hopkins learned the game of politics fairly
well, and he too had ambitions that went beyond the cabinet and
ministership of relief. Striving to please Jersey City's boss, Hopkins gave Hague charge of over 18,000 CWA jobs in 1934. Then
Hopkins appointed Hague's man William Ely as the first director
of WPA in the state. During the thirties New Jersey employed
between 76,000 and 97,000 persons annually through WPA.[13]

That Hopkins lacked the courage or the will to clamp down
on Boss Hague is abundantly clear. New Jersey was one of the
worst states in the nation when it came to political abuses in the
FERA and WPA. Hopkins was inundated with evidence from his
own investigators and from injured citizens. Tons of testimony
and sworn affidavits testify to widespread political coercion. Men
and women who held federal positions in New Jersey were forced

to vote for the machine's candidates; it frequently took connections to find employment in the first place. All jobholders were expected to "tithe" 3 percent of their salaries to the machine at election time. Politics became so flagrantly interwoven in WPA that one director always answered his office phone, "Democratic headquarters!" Even where it was argued that Republicans controlled relief programs, it was well known that Hague actually had his guiding hand in the system because he always rewarded a group of "machine Republicans" who worked faithfully for him by voting in Democratic primaries or becoming "Republicans for Hague."[14]

Hopkins not only ignored the overwhelming evidence of politics in relief programs, he was up to his neck in it himself. New Jersey's state director of relief, William Ely, probably had some wild notion of ultimately building his own machine through the relief program. Consequently, he occasionally circumvented Hague's wishes on patronage if he thought he could do it and not get caught.[15] Hopkins, however, used his personal influence to see that Hague's friends found jobs. In 1936, for example, Hopkins phoned Ely about a gentleman and said, "Frank is very anxious to give him a job." Ely assured the federal minister of relief that "I think maybe we can work it out."[16] Then on another occasion, after a plea from Hague, Harry Hopkins decided to stretch the letter of the law and use WPA funds which were earmarked for labor to buy seats and plumbing for Jersey City's new baseball stadium. Hague knew he was asking Hopkins to put his neck out, but assured him it was for a good cause, inasmuch as the facility was to be named Roosevelt Stadium and the president was going to be present for the grand opening. Once again Hopkins bowed to the throne in Jersey City and pressured Ely to look for a way to pull off the boondoggle for Hague.[17]

Besides these special favors from Hopkins, Frank Hague derived many other benefits from the New Deal. He estimated that his organization gave away approximately $500,000 a month through FERA to hungry families whose heads could not find work. PWA spent over $17,000,000 in Jersey City and Hudson County between 1933 and 1938, and by 1939, WPA had poured nearly $50,000,000 into Hague's city.[18] The machine took political advantage of every dollar and every job which the federal government provided.

To be sure, all the federal support was helpful to the Hague machine, but some was particularly advantageous. The monumental Jersey City Medical Center, for instance, was built largely with grants and loans from PWA. This gigantic complex is composed of seven buildings—the highest of which has twenty-three floors. All in all, the complex encompasses ninety-nine floors with 2,000 beds. At the time of construction it was the third largest hospital in the world.

The Medical Center was Hague's pride and joy. To focus attention on his pet project, he got President Roosevelt to lay the cornerstone in October 1936. The Hudson County boss humbly thanked Roosevelt for the federal funds which were making the project possible. Once the center was finished, though, Hague unabashedly took full credit for extending medical care to everyone who could not afford to pay. He likewise took great delight in attention-getting extravaganzas at the hospital. Without fail, Mayor Hague appeared at the children's ward each Christmas with a lieutenant who was dressed as Santa Claus and bearing gifts for all.[19] With great resourcefulness he squeezed every ounce of political advantage out of the Medical Center. When election time drew near, the boss saw to it that families who had received hospital services were sent bills with enclosed notes informing them that if they went to see their district leader, they could get their bills reduced or completely written off.[20]

In the final analysis, the combined efforts of Roosevelt, Farley, Hopkins, and countless other administrators insured New Deal benefits for the Hague machine. As a careful student of Hague's career concluded, ". . . the fact that the New Deal worked through, rather than in competition with, Frank Hague heightened the dependence of Jersey City families on his organization during the depression decade. The CWA, PWA, WPA, etc., provided resource strength for the Hague machine as it became a vast employment and relief agency."[21]

If it was not for the fact that Roosevelt relied upon the large majorities Hague turned out for him in Hudson County—indeed, Roosevelt could not have carried New Jersey in 1932, 1936, 1940, and again in 1944, without those margins—it is difficult to imagine him putting up with Frank Hague. If he had not found a way to do it earlier, no doubt Roosevelt would have seen the New Jersey Democrat go to federal prison when Farley got the goods on him in 1938—except for the reason he needed him. As we saw in chapter 6 the boss of Jersey City not only delivered the vote, he helped Kelly and Hopkins rig the 1940 convention for the president's third-term nomination.

If Jersey City's mayor had not been a tried and true political asset, he would have gone the route of Kansas City's Tom Pendergast, or at least he would have met the fate of James Michael Curley. This was so because, unlike La Guardia, Kelly, and Flynn—three bosses Roosevelt genuinely liked and enjoyed being with—Frank Hague disgusted him. A key to Roosevelt's personal feelings toward politicians was how often they went for social visits to Hyde Park. While numerous people met the president at his birthplace for brief political meetings, only those Roosevelt thoroughly enjoyed picnicked there or with their families visited overnight. Significantly, Hague attended only one luncheon at Hyde Park. The only time Mrs. Hague and the boss socialized with Roosevelt was on board the cruiser *Indianapolis* in 1934, to review a fleet. Even this outing was a perfunctorily assembled political gathering, which included a substantial number of dignitaries and their wives from New Jersey and New York.[22]

Roosevelt, like many New Dealers, found Hague repulsive. A pushy, arrogant, domineering man, Hague once dictatorially boasted, "I am the law" to a man who questioned the legality of one of his decisions. The New Jersey chieftain had the physique of an athlete, sharp features, and ice-blue eyes. He prided himself on his superb physical condition and enjoyed walking the legs off his associates. His aggressive style complemented his obsessive personality. While he could be flexible when necessary for political advantage, he was dogmatic on several burning issues of the time.

Hague was militantly anticommunist. Typical of the mass Americans he represented, he ignorantly equated communism, socialism, and organized labor. In the name of preserving democracy, he pitched civil liberties to the wind. He said that civil liberties were bunk for anyone "working for the overthrow of the government," and he advocated the establishment of concentration camps in Alaska for American radicals.[23]

Intellectually Frank Hague never grew beyond the elementary grade education he received in Jersey City's Horseshoe district. The capitalist system was good in his eyes, and 100 percent American. To the "Hudson County Hitler," as civil libertarians dubbed him, the Socialist Party and its leader Norman Thomas were subversive. Consequently, when Norman Thomas tried to speak in Jersey City, the Hague-controlled police force stood idly by while angry Hagueites pelted him with rocks and rotten vegetables. Thomas was detained by the police without cause, and the mayor followed this up by banning the socialist's right to speak in Jersey City.[24]

Partly because the local industrialists whom he admired and received so much support from were adamantly opposed to the CIO, Hague did all in his power to oppose its entrenchment in New Jersey. However, this antilabor stand was not merely a facade to win the continued support of the chamber of commerce and industrial magnates. That Hague, the true believer, really viewed it as a communist conspiracy against the American system is evident in his dogged attempt to find evidence of communist connections by scanning the mail of New Jersey's CIO organizers. He believed all organized labor was an anti-American threat, but his most poisonous venom was saved for the CIO. Of the cofounder John L. Lewis, the demagogue from Jersey said he was merely "window dressing"—he was a puppet of the Communist Party.[25]

By the late 1930s Hague openly resorted to police-state tactics of framing his political opponents through the machine-controlled courts. Some apparently innocent persons were jailed for committing no crime other than challenging the "law" of Frank Hague.[26] By 1937 and 1938 President Roosevelt drew increasing criticism from irate citizens, as well as from journalists who spoke for the liberal press.[27] Because of the growing pressure and adverse publicity, it is not at all surprising that Roosevelt allowed a situation to develop which could have worked to his advantage.

It should be recalled that Roosevelt encouraged McKee to enter the mayoralty race in New York City in 1933 to insure Tammany's defeat and, he hoped, to elect La Guardia. But regardless of who won, McKee or La Guardia, Roosevelt came out the winner. He had his hand in the contest, but remained aloof enough to capitalize either way the race went. Then, in 1938 in Missouri, Roosevelt played the game of subtly encouraging

Lloyd Stark in his battle with Pendergast. The president refused, however, to take sides openly until it was clear that Stark had the Missouri Democratic Party fairly well in hand. By 1940 a similar situation developed in New Jersey. Hague was under constant attack for his fascist-style control of Hudson County, but to attack him openly as Farley suggested was dangerous. After all, Hague controlled the Democratic machinery, and without his allegiance Roosevelt could not expect to carry New Jersey.

Roosevelt's plan was to use his secretary of the navy, Charles Edison, son of Thomas A. Edison, to test the anti-Hague sentiment in New Jersey. If Edison could wrest control of the state's pro-Roosevelt forces away from Hague, then Roosevelt could count New Jersey in the Democratic column in elections, yet be rid of the embarrassment of the notorious boss of Jersey City. Roosevelt's New Jersey scheme was tricky. The president had to encourage Edison to launch a reform crusade against the boss, but he had to appear above the battle himself. If Hague thought Roosevelt was in on the coup, then it could cost the president New Jersey's electoral votes in 1940.

The plan seemed especially plausible in light of the Republican victories in New Jersey's off-year elections in 1938. The word which reached the White House was that Republicans won for two reasons. First, citizens were embittered by Roosevelt's attempt to pack the Supreme Court. Second, laborers who ordinarily voted Democratic deserted the party because of Hague's bitter fight against the CIO.[28] This was the first time Hague had not delivered for the New Deal. Was he losing his grip? The best way of finding out, by Roosevelt's way of thinking, was to send up a trial balloon and take a reading.

Domestic circumstances and international events conspired to make Charles Edison the trial balloon. By 1940 Roosevelt knew American involvement in war was imminent. In order to avoid making preparedness appear to be a Democratic Party monopoly, he wanted to appoint Republicans to key defense positions. How fortuitous it was that the secretary of the navy was from New Jersey! If Edison resigned and ran for governor of New Jersey, he could open a cabinet post for a Republican, and at the same time test the wind for breaking Hague's hold on the state.

Like McKee, La Guardia, Farley and Flynn, Charles Edison was taken in by Roosevelt's facade of sincerity. Like so many others, he went out to do battle for Roosevelt only to find it was his own fight: the president's aid would never be forthcoming.

The plan was quickly implemented. Edison entered the Democratic primary, and to the surprise of many received Hague's endorsement. He resigned from the cabinet, and the Republican Frank Knox was appointed. When Roosevelt accepted Edison's resignation, he told him: "I hope you will be elected—and I say this because you have a deep-seated feeling of responsibility to good government and efficient government, which I hope will be recognized by the people of your State."[29] Edison was elected, and Roosevelt sent him a leather notebook as a gift of congratulations.[30]

On the same day in 1940 that Edison was elected governor, Frank Hague delivered a whopping Hudson County vote for Franklin D. Roosevelt. Hague had worked hand-in-hand with Kelly at the national convention to railroad the president through for an unprecedented third term, and he followed up with a huge margin in Jersey City which Roosevelt needed to carry the state.

Soon after Edison entered the governor's mansion, he launched an all-out campaign against Mayor Hague. For the three years of his term he battled the boss, and frequently went to Washington to consult with the president.[31] Although Roosevelt could lend behind-the-scenes encouragement to Edison the trial balloon, he never publicly or openly declared his opposition to Hague.

Charles Edison was in almost every way the antithesis of Hague. He was well educated and reflective, where Hague was ignorant and impetuous. Edison had warm eyes, a sincere smile, and calm and somewhat rounded, soft features, whereas Hague had flashing cold eyes, chiseled features, and the lean, hungry look of a hawk. Edison was a calm, reasonable, and articulate speaker, where Hague was loud, coarse, flamboyant, and impulsive. Edison was an idealist, and his rhetoric was reminiscent of early twentieth-century progressives. He had no organization and made no attempt to build one. Hague, on the other hand, was a calculating realist who understood that organization was essential to winning and keeping office. And he knew, too, that organizations were built on patronage and favors rather than lofty ideals.[32]

Edison also had the severe handicap of being unable to succeed himself as governor after one three-year term because of the state constitution. During his three years in office he managed to embarrass Hague. He got the voters a new constitution, which gave the governor more appointive powers than he had ever had before, and he managed to give the citizens some relief from the extraordinarily high taxes they were paying under the Hague-controlled, highly wasteful government.[33] In the final analysis, though, the trial balloon showed Hague to be indestructible without more drastic action. A journalist with the *New Republic* summed up Edison's impact and Hague's reaction quite well. "After three years in office," wrote Willard Wiener, "Edison has retired to private life. He has materially weakened Hague's stronghold on the people of New Jersey and has provided a favorable opportunity to launch, with federal help, a campaign of liberation. But Hague is still strongly entrenched, with his chief support found in Washington and the Catholic Church, which he has played for all it is worth."[34]

As time passed, it was clear that Hague could be embarrassed but not destroyed. It would have taken action such as Farley suggested in the late 1930s but which Roosevelt would have no part of. In other words, Hague would have to be sent to prison, where he probably belonged—he would have to be handled just like Pendergast—if the Jersey City machine was to be toppled.

But Frank Hague was destined to remain in power until he voluntarily retired from office in 1947 at the age of seventy-one. Roosevelt refused to destroy Hague—which he certainly could have done—because the man who ruled Jersey City politics for nearly half a century was more valuable to the president at the helm of New Jersey's Democratic Party than he was in prison.

Typical of Franklin Roosevelt's lack of loyalty to friends and associates was his final treatment of Charles Edison. If standing by a moral obligation might hurt politically, the man from Hyde Park avoided it. Several months after Edison's gubernatorial term expired, Frank Hague delivered a speech in which he pulled all the stops to smear his erstwhile enemy. The unscrupulous boss, in a bold-faced lie, charged that Edison had been asked to resign from Roosevelt's cabinet in 1940 for "betraying the President."

Edison immediately wired Roosevelt: "In view of previous letters regarding my Navy record from you and others," he begged, "I respectfully request an immediate telegram from you clearly setting forth the falsity of Hague's charges."[35] Roosevelt's secretary, Steve Early, telegraphed Edison that the president had left Washington on top-secret business, and it was too late to take the issue up with him. That was mid-July 1944. Then in late September a disappointed and devastated Edison wrote a note to Early. "I assume by this time that the President is not going to do anything about the Hague matter of which I wrote to you several times in the last couple of months." A notation in the president's file says: "General Watson took this up with the President today [September 30, 1944] and the President answered again in the negative. To be taken up again after the speech of October 5th (perhaps)."[36]

The word "perhaps" was only too telling. Of course, Roosevelt never took it up again. How could he not stand by the man who had loyally served him, the man he had exchanged so many warm notes with and given Christmas gifts to?[37] If Edison had experienced what former favorites La Guardia, Farley, and Flynn had experienced, he would have realized that 1944 was an election year. Roosevelt lacked the courage to do what was morally right. After all, he needed Hague to deliver those sixteen electoral votes from New Jersey one more time.

Perhaps I am unfairly judging Franklin Delano Roosevelt. Those who are inclined to be more charitable toward him may believe that the end justified the means. He was, indeed, in the middle of a war. Maybe he agonized over his obligation to the American people and the free world. Any risk of defeat in 1944 would have, in his eyes, jeopardized this greater obligation. In the last analysis, though, Roosevelt's treatment of Edison is part of a long pattern that goes back to 1933, when he started using associates for his own political advancement. It tells us a great deal about the character of a man who sought the highest office in the United States and made the exceptionally ambitious drive to keep it, not one or two terms, but a third and fourth as well.

8

"THE LAST OF THE OLD-TIME BOSSES"

THE NEW DEAL AND
THE CITY BOSSES IN RETROSPECT

In summer 1947 Frank Hague announced that he was retiring. *Newsweek* observed that "the most dictatorial of the old-style city bosses was following Tom Pendergast, the Kelly-Nash machine, and the Tammany Tiger off the stage. Only Ed Crump of Memphis remained." Chance dictated that the most famous (or infamous) of the nation's city bosses from the Roosevelt era voluntarily retired or were defeated, and then died, in a span of some dozen years. Tom Pendergast led the exit, going to prison in 1939 and living only to 1945. La Guardia, who retired at about the time the Kansas City boss died, lived only two more years. In 1946 Edward Kelly retired, and he died in 1950. Then Edward Flynn, Edward Crump, Frank Hague, and James Michael Curley were laid to rest in 1953, 1954, 1956, and 1958, respectively.

This rapid succession of deaths focused attention on a group of men whose names had been household words throughout America just a few years before. Under pressure to write profound editorials and obituaries in a few hours, news commentators across the land hammered out that well-worn phrase "the end of an era." Not only did the death of each boss mark a watershed in history, but not one of these men died without someone referring to him as "the last of the big-city" or "last of the old-time bosses."[1]

The passing of so many men of power in a relatively short

span of time brought out the usual stream of superficial historical and political analyses. The most common post mortem (and
by far the most popular and long lasting) was the welfare-state
thesis. The story went this way: old-style bosses found their
power among the poor and the immigrants. The urban titans
handed out buckets of coal and baskets of food, and in return
the thankful throng voted the machine slate at election time.
Franklin Roosevelt, however, came along and slew the evil
machines with the thrust of his sword—the welfare state. Social
security, maximum hour and minimum wage laws, prohibition
of child labor, and workingmen's compensation, undermined
the need for bosses. Hence, the passing of the notorious machines
within a decade of Roosevelt's death.

The only problem with this thesis is that it is based on two
erroneous assumptions. The first fallacy is that the machines
found their power primarily among the working classes and the
poor. Not one of these bosses rested solely, or even principally,
on the lower economic class for support. Each one had a broad
base of support coming from all walks of life and every economic
class. The second wrong assumption is that the federal government, by assuming the responsibility for welfare programs, thereby destroyed the machine's useful role as a service institution.
Actually the distribution function was not preempted by the
federal government: under the New Deal many welfare programs
were financed in Washington, but they were *directed* at the local
level.

The evidence shows that where New Deal welfare legislation
had any measurable impact, it was to strengthen individual
urban bosses and their political organizations. Frank Hague, who
had a strong machine in Jersey City by 1932, expanded his
domain to include most of New Jersey by the late 1930s and
early 1940s. When he retired in 1947, he did so voluntarily,
largely because he was seventy-one years old. The New Deal
programs poured millions of dollars into New Jersey, and Frank
Hague used it to strengthen his hold on the entire state.

Dayton David McKean, who observed the Hague machine in
action, put his finger on a vital factor when he said in 1940 that
if the Roosevelt administration "had refused to deal with Hague
its refusal might not have destroyed his organization, but it would

have crippled it and confined it to Jersey City."[2] The key here
is what Roosevelt did. The fate of the city bosses seems to have
been inextricably tied to Roosevelt's policy toward each. The
fate of seven bosses in six cities examined here shows a common
pattern. All machines did not suffer because of the New Deal,
but neither did all prosper. Actually, those bosses smiled upon
by the administration prospered, and those frowned upon withered
and died.

Specifically, Crump and Flynn, like Hague, had well-established
urban machines before 1932. They all cooperated with Roosevelt, and all were showered with money and federal patronage.
Consequently, all of these men remained in power until they
died or retired because of old age or poor health. Kelly and La
Guardia were without established organizations when Roosevelt
was inaugurated, but they showed promise, enthusiastically
supported the president, and proved to his satisfaction that they
were invaluable assets. Roosevelt, in turn, rewarded them with
favors, thus enabling them to entrench firmly their young organizations.

Only two of the famous bosses went down to defeat during
the New Deal era. Both Pendergast and Curley were destroyed
by Roosevelt—but *not* because the welfare programs were erod-
ing the basis of machine politics. Tom Pendergast lost his hold
on Missouri because his machine was thoroughly riddled with
corruption. Pendergast really destroyed himself, although Roosevelt delivered the coup de grace by flooding the state with federal
investigators in a determined effort to send the boss to prison.

James Michael Curley never had a strong organization like
Pendergast, but he did collect large personal followings. During
the heyday of the New Deal he was defeated in four successive
elections—one senatorial, one gubernatorial—and two mayoralty
races. Curley certainly would have been more successful in these
contests if Roosevelt had given some of the patronage and money
to Curley rather than all of it to his opponents. Curley did manage
a stint in Congress in the mid-forties, and he served as mayor of
Boston from 1945 to 1949. The plucky Irishman ran for mayor
three more times, in 1949, 1951, and 1955, but was defeated
each time. After the 1955 battle he retired. He was over seventy
years old, with only three more years to live.

Between Curley's last defeat and his funeral, a talented writer who was familiar with Boston politics, Edwin O'Connor, wrote a novel titled *The Last Hurrah*. Despite his plea inside the cover that "all characters and situations in this novel are fictional, and any resemblance to any person living or dead is purely coincidental," most readers agreed it was a well-told tale based on Jim Curley's rise and fall.

Keep in mind precisely when *The Last Hurrah* was being written. Pendergast had died in 1945, followed by La Guardia in 1947, Kelly in 1950, Flynn in 1953, and Crump in 1954. When the book appeared in 1956, Hague was eighty and dying; only an aged, defeated, and retired Curley remained of the old era. In the concluding pages of the novel two characters, Adam and Jack, try to analyze the defeat of Boss Skeffington. Jack submits that the boss's defeat can be summed up in one word— "Roosevelt."[3]

Adam stared at him. *"Roosevelt?"*
"Sure. F. D. R. Nobody else but. Because he's the man, sport, who really put the skids under your uncle, and he did it years ago. It's just that it took until now to catch up with him."
"I don't get *that* at all," Adam said. "Why Roosevelt?"
"Because," Jack said patiently, "he destroyed the old-time boss. He destroyed him by taking away his source of power. He made the kind of politician your uncle was an anachronism, sport. All over the country the bosses have been dying for the last twenty years, thanks to Roosevelt. Your uncle lasted this long simply because he was who he was: an enormously popular man whose followers were devoted to him. Your uncle wasn't an ordinary boss, sport; the ordinary boss doesn't get that kind of loyalty. But he operated on the old-style principle, and it was just a question of time before what was happening to the rest happened to him, too. . . . Well, of course, the old boss was strong simply because he held all the cards. If anybody wanted anything—jobs, favors, cash—he could only go to the boss, the local leader. What Roosevelt did was to take the handouts out of the local hands. A few little things like Social Security, Unemployment Insurance, and the like—that's what shifted the gears, sport. No need now to depend on the boss for everything; the Federal Government was getting into the act. Otherwise known as a social revolution.

The Last Hurrah was read by millions. It reached the best seller list in 1956, and then Spencer Tracy immortalized Skeffington on the screen. Scholars quickly picked up the O'Connor thesis of the end of old-time bossism. Indeed, an entire issue of the *Annals* of the American Academy of Political and Social Science, titled "City Bosses and Political Machines," reinforced *The Last Hurrah.* Even the insider Rexford G. Tugwell endorsed the thesis in his book *The Brains Trust* (1968).[4] Roosevelt, according to Tugwell,

> ... would show Curry, Ely, Hague, Cermak, Kelly, and Pendergast who was the paramount leader in the party. He would steal their following, force *them* into subordination, make them *his* henchmen. He had begun to show how it could be done. A nationwide system of assistance for those who were dependent on the mean handouts of jobs, favors, food, shelter, or fuel would bring the bosses to heel. They could no longer trade help for votes.

The preceding chapters fail to substantiate this thesis. None of these bosses relied so heavily on indigent support for this to be true. Moreover, the federally-sponsored welfare programs were directed at the local level. Consequently, where welfare was important to a machine before the New Deal, it remained so afterwards as well.

Raymond Moley recognized what so many observers have missed. "Bosses are mortal," he wrote, "but bossism is human nature's eternal summer."[5] The mortality rate of bosses was high in the late forties and fifties because the nation's most notorious city moguls were old men, not because the welfare state had rendered them obsolete. After all, if the welfare state revolutionized local politics, how do we account for the tenacity of Chicago's Richard Daley? He was the third in an unbroken line of successors from Anton Cermak. A number of journalists and political commentators have referred to Daley as an anacronism—the last of the old-time bosses, but that offers little comfort to a host of other politicians in every corner of this country who continually strain and smart under the label of boss.

NOTES

INTRODUCTION

1.   See, for example, "City Bosses and Political Machines," the *Annals of the American Academy of Political and Social Science* 353 (May 1964); Walter Johnson, *1600 Pennsylvania Avenue: Presidents and the People Since 1929* (Boston: Little, Brown, 1963), p. 77; Edwin O'Connor, *The Last Hurrah* (Boston: Little, Brown, 1956); Rexford G. Tugwell, *The Brains Trust* (New York: Viking, 1968), p. 371.

2.   Bruce M. Stave, *The New Deal and the Last Hurrah: Pittsburgh Machine Politics* (Pittsburgh: University of Pittsburgh Press, 1970); Lyle W. Dorsett, *The Pendergast Machine* (New York: Oxford University Press, 1968); Gene Delon Jones, "The Local Political Significance of New Deal Relief Legislation in Chicago, 1933–1940)," Ph.D. dissertation, Northwestern University, 1970; R. J. Connors, "The Local Political Career of Mayor Frank Hague," Ph.D. dissertation, Columbia University, 1966.

1: "AMERICA CALLS ANOTHER ROOSEVELT": The Bosses on the Eve of the National Convention, 1932

1.   Quotations taken from James MacGregor Burns, *Roosevelt: The Lion and the Fox* (New York: Harcourt, Brace & World, 1956), p. 41.

2.   Arthur Mann, *La Guardia Comes to Power: 1933* (New York: Lippincott, 1965), p. 50.

3.   Frank Freidel, *Franklin D. Roosevelt: The Triumph* (Boston: Little, Brown, 1956), pp. 255–60.

4.   For more detail on Flynn's personal and political life, see Edward J. Flynn, *You're the Boss* (New York: Viking, 1947); Richard Rovere, "Profile: Ed Flynn," *New Yorker* 21 (8 September 1945); Raymond Moley, "Boss Flynn Can't Lose," *Saturday Evening Post* 213 (5 October 1940).

5. For detailed accounts of how Hague built his machine and which interest groups supported him, see Mark S. Foster, "The Early Career of Mayor Frank Hague," master's thesis, University of Southern California, 1968; Dayton D. McKean, *The Boss: The Hague Machine in Action* (Boston: Houghton Mifflin, 1940); R. J. Connors, "The Local Political Career of Frank Hague," Ph.D. thesis, Columbia University, 1966.

6. A first-rate study of Cermak, his machine, and his use of power is Alex Gottfried, *Boss Cermak of Chicago: A Study of Political Leadership* (Seattle: University of Washington Press, 1962).

7. President's personal file 955 (MSS, Franklin D. Roosevelt Library, Hyde Park, N. Y.) letter to Louis Howe from A. J. Sabath, 24 September 1932.

8. Gottfried, pp. 210–18.

9. Ibid., pp. 171–75, 305.

10. Interview with James A. Farley, New York City, 28 December 1966.

11. James A. Farley, *Behind the Ballots* (New York: Harcourt, Brace, 1938), p. 121.

12. James A. Farley, *Jim Farley's Story* (New York: McGraw-Hill, 1948), p. 21.

13. Ibid., pp. 21–22.

14. For a fully documented and detailed account of the machine, see Lyle W. Dorsett, *The Pendergast Machine* (New York: Oxford University Press, 1968).

15. Democratic National Committee, 1932 correspondence (MSS, Roosevelt Library) Pendergast quoted in a letter to Roosevelt from Ike Dunlap, 9 July 1931, 1928–33 file D.

16. *Missouri Democrat,* 18 September 1931.

17. Dorsett, chap. 8.

18. J. Joseph Huthmacher, *Massachusetts People and Politics, 1919 to 1933* (Cambridge: Harvard University Press, 1959), p. 14.

19. James Michael Curley scrapbook collection, Holy Cross College, Worcester, Mass., vol. 75.

20. Huthmacher, chaps. 5, 6, 7.

21. President's personal file 1154.

22. See, for example, Ewing Young Mitchell Papers (MSS, Western Historical Manuscripts Collection, University of Missouri, Columbia), letter to E. Y. Mitchell from Curley, 18 April 1932, box 70, fol. 2470.

23. Curley scrapbook collection, vol. 75; Freidel, p. 282.

24. President's personal file 1154, copy of letter to Curley from Roosevelt, 28 April 1932.

25. Curley scrapbook collection, vol. 75.

26. William D. Miller, *Mr. Crump of Memphis* (Baton Rouge: Louisiana State University Press, 1964), p. 173.

27. Democratic National Committee, 1932 correspondence (MSS, Roosevelt Library), copy of letter to Hull from Howe, probably, but it is not typed on the copy, 1 December 1931, box 714.

28. Miller, p. 321.

29. A copy of this pamphlet is in Democratic National Committee correspondence, 1932 (MSS, Roosevelt Library), box 708.

30. Miller, pp. 196–201.

31. President's personal file 1154, letter to James Roosevelt from Curley, 14 November 1931, and attached press release.

2: "THE GREAT ESTRANGEMENT": James M. Curley

1. President's personal file 1154 (MSS, Franklin D. Roosevelt Library, Hyde Park, N. Y.), copy of a letter to Curley from FDR 28 April 1932.
2. J. Joseph Huthmacher, *Massachusetts People and Politics, 1919 to 1933* (Cambridge: Harvard University Press, 1959), 239–40.
3. Curley scrapbook collection, 14–20 September 1932, "Campaigning for Roosevelt in the West." Holy Cross College, Worcester, Mass.
4. See letters and telegrams in president's personal file 1154.
5. President's personal file 1154, telegram to Roosevelt from Curley, 16 February 1933.
6. James Michael Curley, *I'd Do It Again* (Englewood Cliffs, N. J.: Prentice-Hall, 1957), p. 285.
7. Ibid., pp. 247–51.
8. Ibid., pp. 251–52.
9. Ibid., p. 285.
10. Official file 400, Massachusetts (MSS, Roosevelt Library).
11. Examples of Curley's political style and activities can be found in his autobiography *I'd Do It Again,* and in the Curley scrapbook collection at Holy Cross College.
12. Curley, p. 216.
13. Official file 300, Massachusetts, 1933–1945 (MSS, Roosevelt Library).
14. Curley, p. 261.
15. Ibid., p. 262.
16. Alfred B. Rollins, Jr., *Roosevelt and Howe* (New York: Knopf, 1962), p. 327.
17. Curley, p. 286.
18. Curley scrapbook, February 1937.
19. Official file 300, Massachusetts, 1933–1945.
20. President's personal file 1154, 9 January 1936.
21. One of these fireside chat invitations is in official file 300, Massachusetts, 1933–1945, November 1937.
22. Curley scrapbook collection, July–August 1938.
23. Curley, pp. 303–4.
24. *Newsweek,* 28 February 1938.
25. Arthur Macmahon, John D. Millett, and Gladys Ogden, *The Administration of Federal Work Relief* (Chicago: Public Administrative Service, 1941), p.199.
26. For evidence of Curley's use of WPA expenditure cuts for political advantage, see official file 300, Massachusetts, 1933–1945, and Harry Hopkins Papers, box 93, Massachusetts, 1934–1938 (MSS, Roosevelt Library). A copy of the WPA newspaper cited here is in WPA, Massachusetts, 610 Political Coercion (MSS, National Archives), 11 October 1938.
27. WPA, Massachusetts, 610, telegram to Hopkins from Charles V.Coffey, 30 October 1938.
28. Macmahon et al., p. 199.

29.   President's personal file 309, notes between Farley and Roosevelt, 20, 22 December 1939.

30.   Curley, p. 310.

31.   President's personal file 1154, copy of a letter from FDR to Curley, 16 February 1943; letter from Curley to FDR, 26 February 1943.

32.   Curley, p. 327.

33.   Ibid.

34.   *New York Times,* 12 March 1950.

35.   *Nation,* 6 December 1947.

3: "WE MAY HAVE TO BE FOR ROOSEVELT WHETHER WE LIKE IT OR NOT": Edward Crump

1.   President's personal file 3715 (Franklin D. Roosevelt, Library Hyde Park, N. Y.), letter to FDR from McKellar, 30 August 1943.

2.   Although there was an occasional attack on Crump in the slick magazines (see, for example, *Time,* 27 May 1946), most essays praised him for having no scandals and an efficient city government. The typical magazine essay on Crump focused on his charisma and eccentricities rather than on his corruption. See *Life,* 12 August 1946; 26 May 1947; *Newsweek,* 16 August 1948.

3.   Quoted in William D. Miller, *Mr. Crump of Memphis* (Baton Rouge: Louisiana State University Press, 1964), p. 173.

4.   Miller, p. 180.

5.   Quoted in Miller, p. 173.

6.   Miller, p. 179.

7.   Ibid., pp. 180, 186.

8.   Kenneth D. McKellar Papers (Memphis Public Library), letter to McKellar from Crump, 11 April 1939, box 82.

9.   Miller, p. 282.

10.   Official file 300 (Roosevelt Library), Democratic National Committee, Farley correspondence on political trends, Tennessee; president's personal file 5962, copy of notes between McKellar and Roosevelt, 30 August and 14 September 1943; Miller, p. 282.

11.   See, for example, McKellar Papers, letter to McKellar from Crump's secretary E. Humphreys, 25 February 1939, box 82.

12.   Official file 2546 (Roosevelt Library), 23 December 1940; Miller, p. 202.

13.   President's personal file 5962, communications between Roosevelt's office and Crump, 13, 14, 20 March 1945; Miller, pp. 305–6.

14.   James MacGregor Burns, *Roosevelt: The Soldier of Freedom* (New York: Harcourt Brace Jovanovich, 1970), pp. 431–32.

15.   McKellar Papers, letter to McKellar from Crump, 29 May 1944, box 335.

16.   McKellar Papers, copy of letter from Crump to Alfred D. Mynders, 31 July 1944, box 335; *Newsweek,* 18 March 1946.

17.   Official file 300 (Roosevelt Library), copy of letter from Stephen Early to Robert Gates, 16 August 1944, with attached letter and clipping from Gates.

18.   President's personal file 3715, letter to FDR from McKellar, 30 August 1943.

19.   John Dean Minton, "The New Deal in Tennessee, 1932–1938," Ph.D. thesis, Vanderbilt University, 1959, p. 370.

20.   Miller, p. 228.

21.   Democratic National Committee, Farley correspondence, Tennessee, 1936 (Roosevelt Library), letter to Farley from Jere Cooper, 12 August 1936, box 10.

22.   McKellar Papers, correspondence in box 82, dated November 1937.

23.   McKellar Papers, scrapbook 22, clipping dated 10 June 1938.

24.   Official file 300, Democratic National Committee, Farley correspondence on political trends in Tennessee (Roosevelt Library), letter to Farley from Jere Cooper, 12 August 1936.

25.   McKellar Papers, scrapbook 22.

26.   Minton, p. 369.

27.   Ibid., p. 82.

28.   McKellar Papers, box 10; official file 400, Tennessee (Roosevelt Library), letter from secretary of the treasury to Roosevelt, 9 November 1938; Minton, p. 104.

29.   Arthur Macmahon, John D. Millett, and Gladys Ogden, *The Administration of Federal Work Relief* (Chicago: Public Administration Service, 1941), p. 199.

30.   Works Progress Administration, Tennessee, 610 Political Coercion (National Archives); see copy of news release by Hopkins, 29 August 1938; personal interview with Farley, 28 December 1966.

31.   McKellar Papers, letter to McKellar from Harry Berry, 27 April 1939, box 82; see also communications between Berry and McKellar in July 1937, box 82.

32.   McKellar Papers, letter from Crump to McKellar, 2 January 1939, and copy of letter from McKellar to Crump, 5 January 1939, box 22.

33.   Harry Hopkins Papers, narrative field reports, Tennessee (Roosevelt Library), box 82, memo from Gertrude S. Gates, 3 October 1934.

34.   McKellar Papers, correspondence between McKellar and Berry, July 1937, January 1938, June 1938, box 82.

35.   Works Progress Administration, Tennessee, 610 Political Coercion (National Archives), numerous letters dated 1938, including the one quoted here from Willie McGee to Hopkins, 15 July 1938.

36.   McKellar Papers, letter to McKellar from W. C. Cagle, 22 December 1938, box 82.

37.   McKellar Papers, scrapbook 22.

38.   Minton, p. 338; McKellar Papers, box 82, February 1940.

4: "HANDS OFF": Ed Flynn and Fiorello La Guardia

1.   James A. Farley, *Behind the Ballots* (New York: Harcourt, Brace, 1938), p. 156.

2.   Arthur Mann, *La Guardia Comes to Power: 1933* (Philadelphia and New York: Lippincott, 1965), pp. 90–91.

3.   Edward J. Flynn, *You're the Boss* (New York: Viking, 1947), p. 133.

4. Ibid., pp. 133–38.

5. Mann, pp. 95–96.

6. See, for example, president's personal file 880 (MSS, Franklin D. Roosevelt Library, Hyde Park, N. Y.), copy of letter to George Morris from Roosevelt, 10 October 1933; president's personal file 876, copy of letter to Bainbridge Colby from Roosevelt, 28 September 1933.

7. Rexford G. Tugwell, *The Art of Politics* (Garden City and New York: Doubleday, 1958), pp. 123–26, says FDR was for La Guardia all the time.

8. Mann, pp. 66–67.

9. Ibid., p. 67.

10. Farley told me that New York Democrats, including himself, Flynn, and others, resented FDR's all but public endorsement of La Guardia in subsequent elections. They believed Roosevelt should have had more party loyalty and endorsed the Democratic nominees. Personal interview, 28 December 1966.

11. Flynn, p. 138.

12. Personal interview with Farley, 28 December 1966.

13. Flynn, p. 139.

14. A first-rate analysis of La Guardia's machine tactics is in Mann.

15. Personal interview with Farley, 28 December 1966.

16. Richard Polenberg, "Franklin Roosevelt and the Purge of John O'Connor: The Impact of Urban Change on Political Parties," *New York History* 49 (July 1968): 307.

17. Quoted in Tugwell, *Art of Politics,* pp. 92–93.

18. John D. Millett, *The Works Progress Administration in New York City* (Chicago: Public Administration Service, 1938); personal interview with Farley, 28 December 1966.

19. Ibid.

20. Arthur Macmahon, John D. Millett, and Gladys Ogden, *The Administration of Federal Work Relief* (Chicago: Public Administration Service, 1941), p. 199.

21. Charles Garrett, *The La Guardia Years: Machine and Reform Politics in New York City* (New Brunswick: Rutgers University Press, 1961), p. 179.

22. Ibid.

23. Official file 91 (Roosevelt Library), copy of letter to Governor Lehman from E. M. Watson, 23 November 1940; Personal interview with Farley, 28 December 1966.

24. Personal interview with Farley, 28 December 1966.

25. Fiorello La Guardia Papers (New York City Municipal Archives), box 2572.

26. Franklin D. Roosevelt, press conference (Roosevelt Library), 24 October 1941, vol. 18: 256–58.

27. President's personal file 1376, 24 October 1941.

28. See, for example, La Guardia Papers, box 2572, copy of telegram to Roosevelt from La Guardia, 12 August 1936.

29. La Guardia Papers, boxes 819 and 2572.

30. Oral History Project, Columbia University, Charles Poletti and Herbert Lehman, part 2, p. 128; Garrett, p. 259.

31. Tugwell, *Art of Politics,* p. 110.

32. President's personal file 1376, memo to FDR from S. Early, 18 July 1936.

33. Tugwell, *Art of Politics,* p. 92.
34. Garrett, p. 282; Tugwell, *Art of Politics,* p. 109.
35. President's personal file 1376, letter dated 3 February 1943.
36. President's personal file 1376, 6 June 1943.
37. Garrett, pp. 282-83; Tugwell, *Art of Politics,* pp. 109-10.
38. Samuel I. Rosenman, *Working with Roosevelt* (New York: Harper, 1952), p. 123.
39. Oral History Project, Columbia University, Edward J. Flynn, p. 19.
40. President's personal file 1898.
41. Ibid.; see copy of letter from FDR to Flynn, 26 July 1935.
42. President's personal file 1898, copy of letter, 12 August 1940.
43. Oral History Project, Columbia University, Edward J. Flynn, p. 19.
44. James A. Farley, *Jim Farley's Story: The Roosevelt Years* (New York: McGraw-Hill, 1948), pp. 182-83.
45. Flynn, pp. 149-50; Raymond Moley, "Boss Flynn Can't Lose," *Saturday Evening Post* 213 (October 5, 1940).
46. National Archives 610, Political Coercion, New York State.
47. Flynn, p. 150.
48. Moley; Flynn, chaps. 13, 14.
49. Flynn, chap. 14.
50. Ibid.
51. Ibid., pp. 176-77.

5: "HE WAS WITH US FROM THE START": Thomas J. Pendergast

1. Harry Hopkins Papers (MSS, Franklin D. Roosevelt Library, Hyde Park, N. Y.) letter to Hopkins from T. J. Edwards, 9 February 1934, box 81, Missouri reports.
2. For details, see Lyle W. Dorsett, *The Pendergast Machine* (New York: Oxford University Press, 1968).
3. Franklin D. Mitchell, *Embattled Democracy: Missouri Democratic Politics, 1919-1932* (Columbia: University of Missouri Press, 1968), pp. 145-47.
4. *Missouri Democrat,* 27 October 1933.
5. Gloria Winden Newquist, "James A. Farley and the Politics of Victory: 1928-1936," Ph.D. dissertation, University of Southern California, 1966, vol 1, p. 110.
6. Dorsett, p. 104.
7. William Reddig, *Tom's Town: Kansas City and the Pendergast Legend* (New York: Lippincott, 1947), pp. 214-25.
8. Ralph Lozier Papers (MSS, Western Historical Manuscripts Collection, University of Missouri, Columbia), copy of letter to Pendergast from Lozier, 17 April 1933; copy of letter from Farley to Pendergast, 4 May 1933; correspondence between Atterbury and Lozier, August 1933.
9. *Missouri Democrat,* 25 March 1938.
10. Ewing Young Mitchell Papers (MSS, Western Historical Manuscripts Collection), copy of letter from Mitchell to Hopkins, 24 March 1934.
11. Arthur Macmahon, John D. Millett, and Gladys Ogden, *The Administration of Federal Work Relief* (Chicago: Public Administration Service, 1941), p. 199.

12.   The WPA files in the National Archives, which are arranged by states and labeled "Political Coercion," reveal some of the politics and corruption in relief programs.

13.   Lloyd C. Stark Papers (MSS, Western Historical Manuscripts Collection), letter to Stark from Jim Hurst, 11 July 1935, box 309.

14.   Guy B. Park Papers (MSS, Western Historical Manuscripts Collection), copy of letter from Park to Mrs. Hester B. Miller, 21 June 1935, box 56.

15.   Jesse B. Barrett Papers (MSS, Western Historical Manuscripts Collection), photocopy of letter from Truman to L. T. Slayton, 5 February 1935, box 54.

16.   Stark Papers, letter to Stark from Jim Hurst, 27 May 1935, box 308.

17.   Stark was informed as to how the WPA was used in his behalf. See Stark Papers, letter to Stark from A. Moore, 30 January 1936, box 319. Notarized affidavits are in Barrett Papers, dated 16 September 1936, box 53.

18.   Stark Papers, letter to Stark from J. W. Hunolt, 31 October 1936, box 348.

19.   See Stark Papers, files marked "Douglas Campaign," dated May through August 1938.

20.   Dorsett, chap 9.

21.   Stark Papers; see boxes 82, 83, 95, 179.

22.   Stark Papers, letter to Stark from Mrs. McDaniel, 15 September 1938, box 179.

23.   Dorsett, chap. 9.

24.   *Missouri Democrat,* 8 April 1938.

25.   Elmer Irey and William Slocum, "How We Smashed the Pendergast Machine," *Coronet* 23 (December 1947).

26.   Stark Papers; see letters to Stark in boxes 179 and 180.

27.   Stark Papers, boxes 180, 181, 183.

28.   James A. Farley, *Jim Farley's Story: The Roosevelt Years* (New York: McGraw-Hill Book Company, 1948), p. 108.

29.   Dorsett, chap. 9.

30.   Reddig, pp. 385–86; personal interview with Pendergast, 15 March 1961.

31.   Ibid., p. 385.

6: "ROOSEVELT IS MY RELIGION": Edward J. Kelly

1.   "Funeral of a Boss," *Life* 29, 6 (November 1950), 40–41.

2.   President's personal file 3166 (MSS, Franklin D. Roosevelt Library, Hyde Park, N. Y.), letter to Roosevelt from Kelly, no date but stamped received 30 August 1932.

3.   Alex Gottfried, *Boss Cermak of Chicago: A Study of Political Leadership* (Seattle: University of Washington Press, 1962), pp. 308, 316–21.

4.   "Mayor Kelly's Chicago," *Life* 17 (17 July 1944); "Funeral of a Boss"; Irving Dillard, "Chicago as a Sign for 1944," *New Republic* 108 (26 April 1943).

5.   President's personal file 3166, letter to Roosevelt from Kelly, no date, received 30 August 1932; copy of letter to Kelly from Roosevelt, 12 September 1932.

6.   Samuel I. Rosenman, *Working with Roosevelt* (New York: Harper, 1952), p. 123.

7.   President's personal file 2422, digest of letters from Horner to McIntyre, 26 January 1934, and reply dated 7 February 1934.

8.   Gene Delon Jones, "The Local Political Significance of New Deal Relief Legislation in Chicago, 1933–1940," Ph.D. dissertation, Northwestern University, 1970, pp. 88–91.

9.   Ibid., pp. 91–99.

10.   Ibid., chap. 3.

11.   Arthur Macmahon, John D. Millett, and Gladys Ogden, *The Administration of Federal Work Relief,* (Chicago: Public Administration Service, 1941), p. 199; Jones, p. 103.

12.   Harold L. Ickes, *The Secret Diary of Harold L. Ickes,* vol. 1: *The First Thousand Days, 1933–1936* (New York: Simon & Schuster, 1954), pp. 493–94, 557.

13.   Henry Horner Papers (MSS, Library of the Illinois State Historical Society, Springfield), copy of telegram to Lewis from Horner, 7 May 1936.

14.   See, for example, Harry Hopkins Papers (MSS, Roosevelt Library), transcript of Hopkins phone conversation with W. Reynolds, 2 January 1936, box 93.

15.   Democratic National Committee, Illinois (MSS, Roosevelt Library), letter to Farley from Horner, 20 July 1936, box 2.

16.   For evidence of political pressures on WPA workers, see files in the National Archives labeled "Political Coercion, Illinois," and the Horner Papers in files relating to election of 1936; President's personal file 2422, digest of memo to Hopkins, 11 March 1936.

17.   Hopkins Papers, transcript of Hopkins phone conversation with Robert Dunham, 9 December 1936, box 93.

18.   Ickes, vol. 1, p. 463.

19.   Democratic National Committee, Illinois, copy of letter to Kelly from Farley, 17 September 1936. In this letter Farley says they "will do nothing in your County with references to speakers or meetings without first consulting Pat."

20.   Jones, p. 105.

21.   WPA, Illinois, 610 Political Coercion; president's personal file 2422, digest of memo to Hopkins, 11 March, 1936.

22.   Democratic National Committee, Illinois, letter to Farley from Bruce Campbell, 3 October 1936, box 3; letter to Farley from Carter H. Harrison, 18 September 1936, box 3; Horner Papers, letter to Horner from H. M. Adams, 22 November 1935, where Adams sends copy of two-page letter bearing seal which he says will go to 100,000 people in forty-nine counties.

23.   James T. Patterson, *The New Deal and the States: Federalism in Transition* (Princeton: Princeton University Press, 1969), p. 184.

24.   Jones, p. 119; Democratic National Committee, Illinois, letter to Farley from V. Y. Dallman, 9 September 1936, box 2.

25.   Harold L. Ickes, vol. 2: *The Inside Struggle, 1936–1939* (New York: Simon & Schuster, 1954), p. 485.

26.   Searle F. Charles, *Minister of Relief: Harry Hopkins and the Depression* (Syracuse: Syracuse University Press, 1963), pp. 24, 206–19.

27.   John M. Allswang, *A House for All Peoples: Ethnic Politics in Chicago, 1890-1936* (Lexington: University of Kentucky Press, 1971), pp. 161–62, 206–7, "The Kelly-Nash Political Machine," *Fortune* 14 (August 1936); Irving Dillard.

28.   Jones, p. 186.

29.   Ickes, vol. 1, p. 439.

30.   See, for example, Democratic National Committee, Illinois, letter to Farley from Kelly, 24 July 1936, box 2.

31.   President's personal file 3166, copy dated 20 October 1938.

32.   President's personal file 3166, copy of memo to Roosevelt from McIntyre, analyzing Kelly's telegram to FDR 14 October 1938, and suggesting a reply.

33.   Quoted in Jones, p. 195.

34.   Rosenman, p. 123.

35.   President's personal file 3166.

36.   Interview with Farley, 28 December 1966; Ralph Madison, "Letter from Chicago," *New Republic* 112 (23 April 1945).

37.   President's personal file 3166, copy of letter to Kelly from Roosevelt, 1 April 1940.

38.   Edward J. Flynn, *You're the Boss* (New York: Viking, 1947), p. 156.

39.   President's personal file 3166.

40.   Interview with Farley, 28 December 1966.

41.   "Mr. Farley's Successor," *New Republic* 102 (8 April 1940).

42.   Flynn, p. 156.

43.   Interview with Farley, 28 December 1966; Robert E. Sherwood, *Roosevelt and Hopkins* (New York: Grosset & Dunlap, 1950), pp. 173–79.

44.   Dillard.

45.   President's personal file 3166, letter to Roosevelt from Kelly, 5 April 1940.

46.   President's personal file 955, letter to Roosevelt from A. J. Sabeth, 9 April 1938; Farley, *Jim Farley's Story* (New York: McGraw-Hill, 1948), p. 92; Ickes, vol. 3, p. 333; James M. Burns, *Roosevelt: The Lion and the Fox* (New York: Harcourt, Brace & World, 1956), p. 309.

7: "DEMOCRATIC HEADQUARTERS": Frank Hague

1.   Marquis W. Childs, "Dictator—American Style," *Reader's Digest* 33 (August 1938); Jack Alexander, "King Hanky-Panky of Jersey," *Saturday Evening Post* 213 (26 October 1940); Willard Wiener, "Hague is the Law," *New Republic* 110 (31 January 1944); *Literary Digest* 123 (22 May 1937).

2.   Mark S. Foster, "The Early Career of Mayor Frank Hague" master's thesis, University of Southern California, 1968), pp. 5–7; Sutherland Denlinger, "Boss Hague," *Forum* 99 (March 1938).

3.   Dayton D. McKean, *The Boss: The Hague Machine in Action* (Boston: Houghton Mifflin, 1940), pp. 20–27; Denlinger.

4.   Foster, pp. 7–8. McKean, pp. 26–29.

5.   Mark S. Foster, "Frank Hague of Jersey City: The Boss as Reformer," *New Jersey History* 86 (summer 1968).

6.   R. J. Connors, "The Local Political Career of Mayor Frank Hague,"

(Ph.D. thesis, Columbia University, 1966), chap. 3; Wiener; McKean, chaps. 8, 9; Foster.

7. James A. Farley, *Behind the Ballots* (New York: Harcourt Brace, 1938), p. 158.

8. Ibid.

9. President's personal file 1013 (MSS, Franklin D. Roosevelt Library, Hyde Park, N. Y.), letter to Roosevelt from Hague, 24 November 1933.

10. A. Harry Moore Papers (MSS, State Library of New Jersey, Trenton), copy of letter to Joseph Melici from Moore, 12 August 1933, file "Federal 1932–1934."

11. Moore Papers, correspondence in February 1934, in file "Federal 1932–1934."

12. Interview with Farley, 28 December 1966.

13. Connors, p. 130; Arthur Macmahon, John D. Millett, and Gladys Ogden, *The Administration of Federal Work Relief,* (Chicago: Public Administrative Service, 1941), p. 199.

14. WPA, Political Coercion, New Jersey 610 (MSS, National Archives); Narrative field reports, FERA-WPA (MSS, Roosevelt Library), Lorena Hickok to Hopkins, 1936, box 89; Connors, p. 117.

15. Narrative field reports, FERA-WPA, letter to Hopkins from Lorena Hickok, 11 February 1936, box 89.

16. Harry Hopkins Papers (MSS, Roosevelt Library), transcript of phone conversation between Hopkins and Ely, 6 January 1936, New Jersey, box 93.

17. Hopkins Papers, transcript of phone conversations between Hopkins and Hague, 14 January 1937, and Hopkins and Ely, 16 January 1937, New Jersey, box 93.

18. McKean, pp. 103–4.

19. Ibid., chap. 10.

20. Connors, p. 130.

21. Ibid.

22. President's personal file 1013, interview with Farley, 28 December 1966.

23. Bruce Bliven, Jr., "Will the Witness Step Down?" *New Republic* 95 (29 June 1938).

24. "Liberty in Journal Square," *New Republic* 95 (18 May 1938); "Mayor Hague's Long Shadow," *New Republic* 95 (15 June 1938); McAlister Coleman, "Hague's Army Falls Back," *Nation* 147 (26 November 1938).

25. Heywood Broun, "Shoot the Works," *New Republic* 93 (19 January 1938).

26. "Mayor Hague's Long Shadow"; *New York Times,* 18 February 1948; McKean, p. 144.

27. See materials in official file 300, Democratic National Committee, New Jersey 1938, and file 3294 (MSS, both in Roosevelt Library) for correspondence relating to Hague and civil liberties. Among the periodicals which put Hauge under fire and sometimes Roosevelt as well for tolerating him are the *Nation* and the *New Republic.* See especially issues in late 1937 and 1938.

28. Official file 300, New Jersey (MSS, Roosevelt Library), letter from Edward Whalen, 29 December 1938.

29. President's personal file 3159, press release, 24 June 1940.

30. President's personal file 3159, letter from Edison to Roosevelt, 30 December 1940.

31. President's personal file 3159.

32. Copies of Edison's speeches and letters, which give insights into his political views, can be found in the Charles Edison Papers (State Library, Trenton, N. J.).

33. Jack Alexander, "Ungovernable Governor," *Saturday Evening Post* 215 (23 January 1943); Wiener.

34. Wiener.

35. President's personal file 3159, copy of telegram to Roosevelt from Edison, 12 July 1944.

36. President's personal file 3159.

37. Ibid.

8: "THE LAST OF THE OLD-TIME BOSSES": the New Deal and the City Bosses in Retrospect

1. An exception to this was La Guardia. He was usually dubbed a reformer despite the facts that he maintained an organization which was as efficient as any so-called machine and that he used tactics attributed only to bosses. See Arthur Mann, *La Guardia Comes to Power: 1933* (New York: Lippincott, 1965); Lyle W. Dorsett, "The City Boss and the Reformer: A Reappraisal," *Pacific Northwest Quarterly* 63, no. 4 (October 1972).

2. Dayton D. McKean, *The Boss: The Hague Machine in Action* (Boston: Houghton Mifflin, 1940), p. 103.

3. Edwin O'Connor, *The Last Hurrah* (Boston and Toronto: Little, Brown, 1956), p. 374.

4. *Annals,* 353, (May 1964); Rexford G. Tugwell, *The Brains Trust,* (New York: Viking, 1968), p. 371.

5. "What Hague Has Joined Together," *Newsweek* 29 (16 June 1947).

SOURCES

The Franklin D. Roosevelt Library at Hyde Park, New York, houses several collections which were central to this study. The president's personal file and the official files contain correspondence and memoranda relating to all the bosses, and especially to Roosevelt's contacts with them. The files of the Democratic National Committee, arranged geographically by states and chronologically by presidential election campaigns, are invaluable in describing how the organizations were structured and how they functioned at the city and state levels. The Harry Hopkins Papers not only contain correspondence between Hopkins and key figures in this study, but transcripts of important telephone conversations as well.

To my knowledge, the first scholar to utilize the "Political Coercion" file 610 in the Works Progress Administration records in the National Archives was Searle F. Charles. His book *Minister of Relief: Harry Hopkins and the Depression* (1963) suggests some of the ways the WPA was abused politically, and it inspired me to make a search (which proved to be quite fruitful) of the documents relating to Massachusetts, Missouri, Tennessee, Illinois, New York, and New Jersey.

Beyond these key collections at the Roosevelt Library and the National Archives, collections in each of the states proved useful. The James M. Curley scrapbook collection at Holy Cross College in Worcester, Massachusetts, is extensive and well organized chronologically. Primarily newspaper clippings relating to Curley, it saved me weeks of newspaper research and added much to what I found in Curley's autobiography *I'd Do It Again* (1957), and two excellent books, *Massachusetts People and Politics, 1919–1933* (1959) by J. Joseph Huthmacher, and *The Political Cultures of Massachusetts* (1965) by Edgar Litt.

The papers of Senator Kenneth McKellar at the Memphis Public Library are rich in McKeller's correspondence with Crump and important political figures in Washington, D. C. This large collection fleshed out my story, and added an important dimension to materials included in William Miller's biography of Edward Crump, *Mr. Crump of Memphis* (1964), and a careful

Vanderbilt University Ph.D. thesis by John Dean Minton, "The New Deal in Tennessee, 1932–1938" (1959).

The Fiorello La Guardia Papers at the New York City Municipal Archives enhanced my New York chapter, as did the Edward J. Flynn, Charles Poletti, and Herbert Lehman transcripts in the Columbia University Oral History Project. A personal interview with James A. Farley enlightened me considerably about the complexity of New York politics in the thirties, and about Roosevelt's and Farley's involvement with the bosses outside of New York as well. Edward Flynn's autobiography *You're the Boss* (1947) is more useful than most autobiographies. Arthur Mann's two volumes on La Guardia were indispensable to this study. Volume 2, *La Guardia Comes to Power, 1933* (1965), is the most insightful work ever done on the "machine" side of "reform" in New York. Charles Garrett's *The La Guardia Years: Machine and Reform Politics in New York City* (1961) is a long, poorly conceived volume of very limited use.

The research for my own book *The Pendergast Machine* (1968) is the nucleus of the chapter on Missouri. The papers of Ralph Lozier, Jesse Barrett, Lloyd Stark, Guy Park, and Ewing Young Mitchell, all housed at the Western Historical Manuscripts Collection, State Historical Society of Missouri, Columbia, were absolutely invaluable to me, as was a fine monograph by Franklin D. Mitchell, *Embattled Democracy: Missouri Democratic Politics, 1919–1932* (1968). Mitchell is the only scholar who has been given complete access to the James A. Reed Papers, which are in the possession of Senator's Reed's widow. The late William Reddig's book *Tom's Town: Kansas City and the Pendergast Legend* (1947) still stands as one of the best books available on Missouri politics in the Pendergast era.

The Henry Horner Papers at the library of the Illinois State Historical Society were extremely useful to me in learning how the opposition assessed the strengths and weaknesses of Edward Kelly's organization. A well-researched and well-conceived Northwestern University Ph.D. dissertation by Gene Delon Jones, "The Local Significance of the New Deal Relief Legislation in Chicago: 1933–1940" (1970), augmented my work, as did *The Secret Diary of Harold L. Ickes*, volume 1 (1954); *A House for All Peoples: Ethnic Politics in Chicago, 1890–1936* (1971) by John M. Allswang; and Alex Gottfried's first-rate biography of Kelly's predecessor and mentor, *Boss Cermak of Chicago: A Study of Political Leadership* (1962).

Despite the fact that a member of the library staff at the State Library of New Jersey in Trenton assured me there would be no Hague material in Governor A. Harry Moore's papers, I searched the collection anyway and found it rich in materials on Hague and New Jersey politics. The Charles Edison Papers in the same library are well ordered, apparently complete, and essential to anyone interested in anti-Hague politics. Besides these two manuscript collections, two scholars have studied Hague's machine and made some significant contributions: Mark S. Foster, "The Early Career of Mayor Frank Hague," master's thesis, University of Southern California, 1968; and R. J. Connors, "The Local Political Career of Frank Hague," Ph.D. dissertation, Columbia University, 1966. Finally, a political scientist, Dayton D. McKean, wrote an attack on Hague during the 1940 campaign. Entitled *The Boss: The Hague Machine in Action* (1940), this is a polemical treatise, but it contains some valuable material and insights.

INDEX